In Defense of The Holy Trinity

A Concise Rebuttal of Arianism, Oneness Theology, and Unitarianism

Sonny L. Hernandez

Soli Deo Gloria!

Look to the glorious gospel, and you will see
God is not unipersonal, but a blessed Trinity
The elect of God for whom Christ died can see
In the Godhead, there is always perfect harmony

To my friend, Ricky Hill,
"For I reckon that the sufferings of this present time are
not worthy to be compared with the glory which shall be
revealed in us" (Romans 8:18).

In loving memory of
Amanda and James Richard ("J. R.") Hill V

χάρις ὑμῖν καὶ εἰρήνη ἀπὸ Θεοῦ πατρὸς ἡμῶν
καὶ Κυρίου Ἰησοῦ Χριστοῦ.

Table of Contents

1. Christ is God from the essence of the Father,
He is the second person of the Trinity
Jesus Christ is the intrinsic form of Yahweh,
Being the effulgence of God's glory

2. The two-natured person of the Son, Jesus
God the Logos was made flesh and dwelt among us
begotten before time, not made or created
God in three persons are co-glorious

3. He is not divided into two-persons,
but one and the same, Logos, and the sinless lamb
The incarnate Savior has two-minds and two-wills,
Before Abraham was, Christ said, "I AM"

4. Exalted Christ, fully man and fully God,
preexistent Son who predates His creation
The resurrected Son of God died for His sheep
His elect are guaranteed salvation

5. The Son is consubstantial with the Father,
He is God's beloved Son, full of blessedness
Salvation and assurance are for God's elect,
grounded in Christ's imputed righteousness[1]

"Christological Hymn"
Written by Sonny Hernandez

---

[1] References: Holy Bible, Athanasian Creed, Nicene Creed, Chalcedonian Creed. Sing this hymn to the tune of "Holy, Holy, Holy."

Preface

The doctrine of the Trinity is an essential of the Christian faith, and it is absolutely necessary to everlasting salvation that one rightly believes in "one God in Trinity and the Trinity in unity" (Athanasian Creed).

There are serious implications for denying the plurality of distinct and consubstantial persons in the Godhead. Rejecting the Trinity is tantamount to rejecting God and the gospel, because the one true God is Triune, and the true gospel is grounded in the Trinity.

In Defense of the Trinity is an exegetical book on the Tri-personality of God, and it is a concise refutation of Arianism, Oneness theology, and Unitarianism.[2] This book is not an exhaustive study on the multi-personality of God, but it does serve as an evangelistic resource for Christians, and the local church.

As a disclaimer, this book does not address every distinctive of Arianism, Oneness Theology, or Unitarianism; nor does this book assume that these worldviews agree on every doctrinal point. For example, many advocates of Oneness Pentecostalism

---

[2] Regarding definitions, Arianism is a denial of the preexistence and deity of Christ. Oneness Pentecostalism teaches that the Father, the Son, and the Spirit refer to the same *hypostasis*. Additionally, the reference of *Unitarianism or Unitarians* in this book points to those who deny the Trinity, not the Unitarian Universalist denomination.

reject the perseverance of the saints, but many do not.

Therefore, the purpose of this book is not to address every distinctive or worldview that denies the multi-personality of God, but to defend the Trinity, and refute those who believe God is unipersonal, not Tri-personal, which is a conviction held by Arians, Oneness Pentecostals, and Unitarians.

The Triune God will deliver His elect, or He will harden the reprobate, in accordance with His good pleasure, and immutable will. This is because the **Father** chose the elect, not reprobate, the **Son** died for the sheep, not goats, and the **Holy Spirit** will seal the invisible church, not those outside of it.

May God's will be done, for His glory!

Sonny L. Hernandez
Pastor, Trinity Gospel Church, KY
TrinityGospelChurch.com

Chapter 1

Defending the Trinity, and Refuting Unitarianism

The multi-personality of God and the coessential deity of Christ, God the *Logos*, are essentials of the Christian faith. True Christians worship "one God in Trinity and the Trinity in Unity" (excerpt from the Athanasian Creed), because they believe the one true God exists in a plurality of distinct and consubstantial *hypostases* or persons.

But modalists think God is a singular person, who can be seen throughout Scripture in different modes, meaning the Father, the Son, and the Spirit are referring to the same *hypostasis*. Put another way: these modern-day Sabellians think Jesus is either an abstraction in the mind of God, or the Father suffered and died on the cross in the mode of Christ.

Since false teachers reject the plurality of persons in the Godhead, the preexistence and full deity of Christ, and the dual nature of the person of the Son who became incarnate, this chapter will provide concise refutations to a few proof texts that Unitarians will twist.

I. Triadic Formula

Oneness theologians do not believe Matthew 28:19 is a Triadic formula, because "name" is singular, not plural. But this does not mean God is not multi-personal. Trinitarian scholars have historically and exegetically demonstrated that the noun *sem* [LXX: "onoma"; trans. "name"] in Genesis 11:4 is singular, but points to many.

The context of Matthew 28:19 is problematic for those who think there is not a plurality of personal or hypostatical distinctions. Linguistically, in this passage, the conjunction *kai* ("and") is connective, not ascensive, and the definite article ("the") stresses particularity.[3]

Even if one does not embrace the Granville Sharp Rule,[4] it's impossible to deny the Trinal distinction of persons in Matthew 28:19, because each noun (Father, Son, Ghost) shares the same case (genitive), each noun is connected by the copulative or conjunction ("kai"), and each noun has the article ("the").

Therefore, the following grammatical construction [def art + noun (gen) + conj + def art + noun (gen) + conj + def art + noun (gen)] in Matthew 28:19 proves the one true God (ousia) exists in three distinct persons, i.e., the Father, the Son, and the Spirit.

Regarding the Tri-personality of God, the

---

[3] Joseph H. Thayer, *Thayer's Greek-English Lexicon of the New Testament* (Peabody, MA: Hendrickson Publishers), 315-317. Reprinted form the fourth edition originally published by T. & T. Clark, Edinburgh, 1896, with *Strong's* numberings added by Hendrickson Publishers.

[4] Daniel B. Wallace, *Greek Grammar Beyond the Basics: An Exegetical Syntax of the New Testament* [GGBB] (Grand Rapids, MI: Zondervan, 1996), 270-290.

Father is not ontologically greater than the Son, the Son is not eternally subordinate to the Father, the Spirit is not inferior to the Father or Son; nor is one person more glorious than the others. Since all three persons share the same undivided essence, they are co-equal, co-glorious, and co-eternal with each other. Therefore, the Trinity of persons in the Godhead are to be equally worshiped and served. Praise the Triune God!

II. "His Son" & "True God"

Moreover, since "God" is articular and "Son" is anarthrous in Hebrews 1:1-2, Unitarians think the absence of the article for "Son" means Christ and the Father refer to the same person. But the context of Hebrews 1 proves "*o Theos*" (1:1) and "*en uio*" (1:2) do not refer to the same, but distinct persons.

Grammatically, "His Son" indicates the consubstantiality of the Son, and many exegetes would agree. For example, Leon Morris said that "*en uio*" (1:2) means, "...in one who has the quality of being Son" and "it is the Son's essential nature that is stressed."[5]

Christ, the preexistent Son of Man, was co-glorious with the Ancient of Days, and He became flesh, but without sin. As the God-man or *Theanthropos*, He is the being of all beings, and the apocalyptic judge of all humanity.

---

[5] Leon Morris, *Hebrews*, in vol. 12 of *The Expositor's Bible Commentary*, ed. Frank E. Gaebelein and J. D. Douglas (Grand Rapids, MI: Zondervan, 1981), 13.

Furthermore, 1 John 5:20 says, "…even in his Son Jesus Christ. **This is the true God**, and eternal life" (emphasis mine). Consequently, many Unitarians and even scholars have argued that "true God" refers to the Father, not the Son, because Christ is not regarded as *alethinos Theos* in Scripture.

But the only way to know whether *true God* refers to the Father or Son is to examine the context and determine what's the antecedent of *outos* or "this." This is not a difficult task, especially since the dative *Xristo* is immediately followed by the demonstrative pronoun *outos*, and both "Christ" and "this" agree in number (singular) and gender (masculine).

Nonetheless, the persons in the Godhead are distinct, not divided, and they share the same undivided essence. Therefore, each person is wholly God, and each person should be referred to as the "true God."

Christ is the true God, and His gospel teaches that He is in every way God, but distinct from the Father, and the person of the Son became incarnate. He died a substitutionary and propitiatory death for the sheep, not goats, and He resurrected for the elect, not reprobate.

III. The Spirit is a person, not impersonal force

Lastly, false teachers think the Holy Spirit denotes an impersonal force, not a person, but they are not hard to refute. Many of them will adamantly argue that only a human being is a person, and Scripture never teaches that the Spirit is a person. When they make these imbecilic assertions, ask them to read Acts 13:2. This text states, "...the Holy Ghost said, 'Separate **me** Barnabas and Saul for the work whereunto **I** have called them'" (emphasis mine). Then ask them, "If the Spirit is not a person, why does the Spirit refer to Himself in the first person" ("I" and "me")? Only a self-aware, rational, and moral individual or *hypostasis* can say "I" or "me." Again, heretics are not hard to refute.

Closing

Arius, a fourth century heretic, believed there was a time when Christ was not. Similarly, Eusebius of Nicomedia agreed with Arius' gross conviction, indicating that he also denied the preexistence and coessential divinity of Christ, God the *Logos*. Eusebius' Christology was not overlooked, but was addressed by the bishops, who said: "You lie!" "Blasphemy!" "Heresy!"

According to a notable church historian, "We are told that his speech was snatched from his hand, torn to shreds, and trampled underfoot."[6] This is exactly how Christians should respond to heresies that deny the multi-personality of God, or the completed and saving work of Christ, who is both God and man simultaneously, yet one person.

---

[6] Justo L. Gonzalez, *The Story of Christianity: The Early Church to the Dawn of the Reformation.* Vol. 1. (New York, NY: Harper Collins, 1984), 164.

Chapter 2

An Exegetical Summary of Christology

False teachers reject the Tri-personality of the one true God, the preexistence of the Son, the dual nature of Christ, and full deity of the person of Christ who became incarnate.

Therefore, the purpose of this chapter is to provide a concise and exegetical overview of several biblical texts, which undeniably stress the multi-personality of God, and the coessential divinity of the Son.

I. John 1:1

Unitarians deny the preexistence and full deity of Christ, but the stative verb *en* ("was") in John 1:1 is in the imperfect tense, which signifies that Christ, the *monogenes Theos*, is eternally self-existent and uncaused.

Exegetically, John 1 not only teaches that Christ predates creation [Gk: "en"; Eng: "was" (John 1a); imperfect tense indicates "…continuous timeless existence"],[7] but it also reveals that Christ is wholly God, but distinct from the Father.

II. John 1:14

---

[7] Cleon L. Rogers Jr. and Cleon L. Rogers III, *The New Linguistic and Exegetical Key to the Greek New Testament* (Grand Rapids, MI: Zondervan Publishing House, 1998), 175.

Christ is the second person of the Trinity, and He is consubstantial, coessential, or *homoousios* [homo: same + ousios: substance] with the Father. Jesus possessed and exercised the fullness of deity or divine attributes (before, during, and after the incarnation).[8]

The Son of God was begotten [mono: only + genes: kind or class] of the Father before time, not made or created, and was made flesh [Gk: "sarx egeneto" (John 1:14); lit., "to become, be made"].[9]

Christ is wholly God and wholly man, with two distinct, unmingled, and inseparable natures. Therefore, He is one person (hypostasis), not two (Nestorian heresy), and He has two wills, not one [Monothelitism heresy: monos (single) + thelo (will)].

Monothelitism [monos: single + thelo: will] is an insurmountable trap, and those who affirm it cannot explain how Christ is all knowing (Matthew 9:4; 12:25; Mark 2:8; Luke 6:8; 9:47; 10:22; John 2:24-25; 6:64; 10:15; 16:30; 21:17; Revelation 2:23), but did not know the day or the hour (Matthew 24:36; Mark 13:32).

When the preexistent ["en" ("was"), lit. predates creation] Christ "became flesh" ["sarx

---

[8] During the incarnation, Christ, God the *Logos*, exercised the plentitude or *pleroma* of deity, but many kenotic or sub-kenotic theoreticians think the Son only had restricted access to all of the divine attributes. Let God be true, and every man a liar.

[9] Thayer, *Thayer's Greek-English Lexicon of the New Testament*, 115.

egeneto"], His divinity and humanity were inseparably or indissolubly united, without contradiction. So the person of Christ has two wills and two minds. For example, Matthew 26:39 says, "...O my Father, if it be possible, let this cup pass from me: nevertheless not as I will (human will), but as thou wilt (divine will)."

III. John 8:58

According to John 8:58, Christ said "...Before Abraham was (prin abraam genesthai), I am" (ego eimi). The verb *genesthai* is an aorist, which signifies that Abraham had a beginning, whereas *ego eimi* points to Exodus 3:14, which indicates the essence or divinity of the one true God who subsists in a plurality of persons.

"I am" refers to the absolute sovereignty of God, and it denotes Yahweh's eternality, self-existence, and immutability.[10] Therefore, when Christ said "*ego eimi*," He was literally declaring to be the one true God or the Yahweh of the Old Testament (OT).

Christ was also maintaining that He is the ultimate standard of all standards, the being of all beings, the sole ultimate cause of all things, and the source or foundation of all blessings.

---

[10] John Gill, "*Exodus*," in *The Baptist Commentary Series*: *John Gill's Exposition of the Old and New Testaments*, vol. 1, Genesis to Numbers (1809; repr., Paris, AR: The Baptist Standard Bearer, 2006), 329. All subsequent references of Gill's commentaries will be cited as: Gill, *Baptist Commentary Series*, Hebrews 1 (for example).

IV. John 20:28

Unitarians don't believe that Christ is both Lord and God, but Thomas said in John 20:28, "... My Lord [definite article: o ("the") + Kyrios ("Lord")] and my God" [definite article: ὁ ("the") + Theos ("God")]. Based on the context of John's gospel (John 20:19-29), Thomas is without a doubt speaking to Jesus in John 20:28.

V. Philippians 2:6/Hebrews 1:3

There are two significant present tense participles that need to be examined: "[Who], being ("hyparchon") in the form of God…" (Philippians 2:6), and "[Who] being ("on") the brightness of his glory…" (Hebrews 1:3).

The participles are preceded by the relative pronoun ("who"), which undoubtedly refers to Christ [pronoun-antecedent agreement (number/gender)], God the *Logos*, and each verb ("being") is in the present tense. Exegetically, these participles emphasize the Son's continuous being or existence. This means the preexistent Christ has and will always be the intrinsic form of YHWH, and the *doxa* of God.

VI. Colossians 1:16

There are many EFS (Eternal Functional Subordination) or ERAS (Eternal Relations of Authority and Submission) exegetes who argue that Christ, the *monogenes Theos*, is eternally subordinate to the Father.

What exegetical arguments are used to support the notion of EFS or ERAS? As an example, some scholars insist that the grammatical construction *dia* + genitive refers to the intermediate agent (The Son), not ultimate, whereas *upo/apo/para* + genitive points to the ultimate agent (The Father).

Yes, *dia* + genitive refers to Christ. Both John 1:3 and Colossians 1:16 teach that all things were made "by Him" (dia + genitive autou). The New Testament (NT) also reveals that the construction *apo* + genitive points to the Father. Revelation 12:6 states, "where she hath a place prepared ***of God***…" (apo + genitive *tou Theou*, emphasis mine). But do these grammatical constructions indicate that Christ is the intermediate agent (not ultimate), or eternally subordinate to the Father? Absolutely not!

The preposition *dia* + genitive *autou* not only indicates intermediate, but also ultimate. Before addressing how dia + gen also refers to the ultimate agent, one must carefully examine how notable scholars have defined intermediate agent, since this is who most EFS or ERAS advocates appeal to. For example, Wallace defined intermediate agent (dia + gen) as "Indicating the person who carries out the act **for the ultimate agent**."[11]

But the context of Colossians 1:16 [prep: di + gen: autou], which refers to Christ, does not indicate that the Son carried out the act for the Father, **but for Himself**. See Paul's exegesis: "By Him" [preposition (en) + dative (auto)], "through Him" [preposition (di)

---

[11] Wallace, *GGBB*, 747, emphasis mine.

+ genitive (autou)], and "for Him" [preposition (eis) + accusative (auton)]. This text literally means that Christ conceived, created, and controls all [nuet. ta panta] things for Himself.

VII. 2 Peter 1:1/2 Corinthians 13:14

Read 2 Peter 1:1 ("...through the righteousness of God and our Savior Jesus Christ"), and examine the following grammatical construction: "...*tou* [def art: "the"] + *Theou* [noun: "God"] + *kai* [conj: "and"] + *Iesou Xristou*" [noun: "Jesus Christ"].

According to the Granville Sharp Rule, when the conjunction *kai* ("and") connects both nouns of the same case, and the preceding noun has the article ["tou": "the"], while the latter does not, this basically means that both nouns are synonymous.[12]

Additionally, when the copulative *kai* connects nouns of the same case, and each case has a definite article, each noun refers to distinct and divine *hypostases*, i.e., the Father, the Son, and the Spirit.

For example, see the following construction in 2 Corinthians 13:14: definite article ("the") + noun ("Jesus") + conjunction ("and") + definite article ("the") + noun ("God") + conjunction ("and") + definite article ("the") + noun ("Spirit").

Those who don't understand the biblical doctrine of the Trinity don't truly know God or His gospel, because the one true God of the Bible subsists

---

[12] Ibid., 270-290.

in a plurality of distinct and consubstantial persons, and the gospel is grounded in the Trinity. So giving adulation or praise to anyone else is gross idolatry, and *will worship* (ethelothreskeia).

How is "will worship" defined? Definition of *ethelothreskeia* [Gk: ἐθελοθρησκεία; Eng: "will worship" (Colossians 2:23, KJV)]: superstitious worship, invented by imprudent men, who think worship must be entertaining or relevant, and not explicitly regulated by the one true God.

While many are vexed about the doctrine of the Trinity or Christology, no one can deny the existence of the one true God who is multi-personal, not unipersonal. Romans 1:21 proves that all men—head for head—have an instinctual knowledge of God's existence. This text states, "Because that, when they knew God…" (dioti gnontes ton Theon). The verb *gnontes* ("knew") is a participle, and it means to perceive or to be intellectually aware.[13]

Additionally, the Greek NT includes the definite article ("…ton Theon"), which stresses particularity. So Paul was literally teaching that all men are intuitively aware of the God, not a god. This is why Psalm 14:1 states, "The fool hath said in his heart, 'There is no God…'"

Closing

All doctrines that reject the person of the Son,

---

[13] Thayer, *Thayer's Greek-English Lexicon of the New Testament*, 117-118.

or the dual nature and full deity of Christ, or the unity
and plurality of the Godhead, must be condemned as
heresy.

Chapter 3

A Christological Outline of Hebrews 1

The prologue of Hebrews 1 is a Christological treatise, which underscores the distinction of persons in the Godhead, the nature of God, the full deity of Christ, the eternality of the Son, the supremacy of the Savior, and the glory of the *Logos*.

This chapter poses a major problem for those who don't believe three distinct persons share one *homoousion* (same essence) in the Godhead, or that Christ, the preexistent *Logos*, is *"tou megalou Theou kai soteros emon Iesou Xristou"* ("...the great God and our Savior Jesus Christ," Titus 2:13). The purpose of this chapter is to provide an exegetical and Christological outline of Hebrew 1.

I. Christ is distinct from the Father (vv. 1-2)

> God, who at sundry times and in divers manners spake in time past unto the fathers by the prophets, Hath in these last days spoken unto us by his Son, whom he hath appointed heir of all things, by whom also he made the worlds;

a. *Distinct, not divided* ("o Theos"/"uio")

False teachers slavishly think the Father and Son refer to the same person. But the context of Hebrews 1 proves *o Theos* ("the God") and *uio*

("Son") are distinct, and not referring to the same *hypostasis*.

Even though *uio* is anarthrous, some advocates of Oneness theology will say this contextually means Christ is either an abstraction in the mind of God, or is simply the Father in the mode of the Son.

But the absence of the article does not support Unitarian dogma, because *uio* is a qualitative noun that stresses the essence of the Son. Wallace explained that the force of *uio* in Hebrews 1:2 is "clearly qualitative,"[14] which "…places the stress on quality, nature, or essence."[15]

b. *Supremacy over all* ("kleronomon")

According to the author of Hebrews, the Father appointed the Son as the *kleronomon* or heir of all things. Thayer argued that the accusative *kleronomon* means, "in Messianic usage, one who receives his allotted possession by right of sonship."[16] This commentary indicates that all men and all things are subjugated to Christ.

Christ, the preexistent Son of Man, was co-glorious with the Ancient of Days, and He became flesh, without sin, in accordance with His humanity. As the God-Man or *Theanthropos*, He is the being of

---

[14] Wallace, *GGBB*, 245.
[15] Ibid., 244.
[16] Thayer, *Thayer's Greek-English Lexicon of the New Testament*, 349.

all beings, and the apocalyptic judge of all humanity. Thus, all things are held in subjection to His will.

c. *Agent of creation* [prep. "di" + gen. "ou"]

The last clause of Hebrews 1:2 states, "…by whom also he made the worlds." "By whom" [prep. di + gen. ou] is a grammatical construction that is not foreign to scholars. Murray Harris said the "prep. + gen. can express ultimate cause…,"[17] and Wallace believes the prep. + gen. refers to the intermediate agent or the person who "carries out the act for the ultimate agent."[18] Examine how the prep. + gen. can also be seen in the following texts:

- **John 1:3:** "All things were made **by him** [prep. di + gen. autou], and without him was not any thing made that was made" (emphasis mine).

- **Colossians 1:16:** "…all things were created **by him** [prep. di + gen. autou], and for him" (emphasis mine).

The context of these passages do not teach that Christ carried out the act for the Father (intermediate), but for Himself (ultimate). Thus, "by whom" [prep. di + gen. ou] in Hebrews 1:2 indicates Christ is the ultimate cause or the agent of creation.

---

[17] Murray J. Harris, *Colossians*, in *Exegetical Guide to the Greek New Testament. Colossians and Philemon.* 2nd Ed. (Nashville, TN: B&H Publishing Group, 2010), 42.
[18] Wallace, *GGBB*, 747.

II. Christ shares the same essence
as the Father (v. 3)

> Who being the brightness of his glory, and the express image of his person, and upholding all things by the word of his power, when he had by himself purged our sins, sat down on the right hand of the Majesty on high:

a. *Important participle* ("on")

There are many significant theological points that need to be addressed in Hebrews 1:3, mainly "being," "brightness," "express image," and "nature" ("os **on apaugasma** tes doxes kai **character** tes **hypostasis** autou," emphasis mine).

Regarding the antecedent of *os* or "who," the relative pronoun *os* refers to *uio*, because "*Son*" is the preceding noun, and "who" and "Son" agree in gender (masculine) and number (singular).

The present participle *on* ("being") indicates a continuous state of being, or "absolute and timeless existence."[19] This verb is critical, because it emphasizes the nature or substance of the Son, God the *Logos*.

b. *Effulgence of God* ("apaugasma")

As the eternally begotten Son, not made or created, Christ is the *apaugasma* or effulgence of

---

[19] Rogers & Rogers, *The New Linguistic and Exegetical Key to the Greek New Testament*, 516.

God. Put another way, the shekinah glory or brightness of *Yahweh* is manifested in the person of the Son. The *Logos* is the *doxa* of God, but distinct from the Father.

c. *Character of God* ("charakter")

The English word *character* derives from the Greek word *charakter*, which can only be seen in Hebrews 1:3. F. F. Bruce asserted that character "(from the verb charasso in the sense "engrave") is used especially of the impression or stamp on coins and seals,"[20] and Richard Phillips said *charakter* means Christ "bears God's image."[21]

d. *Nature of God* ("hypostasis")

According to notable Lexicons, the noun *hypostasis* can be translated as person, but the context of Hebrews 1:3 stresses "the essential or basic structure/nature of an entity, substantial nature, essence, actual being, reality…",[22] or the "the substantial quality, nature, of any person or thing."[23]

---

[20] F. F. Bruce, *The Epistle to the Hebrews*, in *The New International Commentary on the New Testament: The Epistles to the Colossians, to Philemon, and to the Ephesians* (Grand Rapids, MI: William B Eerdmans Publishing Company, 1990), 48.

[21] Richard D. Phillips, *Hebrews*, in *Reformed Expository Commentary* (Phillipsburg, NJ: P&R Publishing, 2006), 20.

[22] Walter Bauer, Frederick W. Danker, William F. Arndt and F. Wilbur Gingrich., *A Greek-English Lexicon of the New Testament and Other Early Christian Literature*, 3rd Ed. (Chicago, IL: University of Chicago Press, 2000), 1040.

[23] Thayer, *Thayer's Greek-English Lexicon of the New*

Christ is the intrinsic form of God, and the embodiment of *Yahweh*. This is why Jesus said, "…he that hath seen me hath seen the Father" (John 14:9).

For an exegetical commentary on the remainder of Hebrews 1:3, see A. T. Robertson's Word Pictures in the NT:

> **And upholding** (φερων τε). Present active participle of φερω closely connected with ων (being) by τε and like Colossians 1:17 in idea. The newer science as expounded by Eddington and Jeans is in harmony with the spiritual and personal conception of creation here presented.

> **By the word of his power** (τω ρηματ της δυναμεως αυτου). Instrumental case of ρημα (word). See Hebrews 11:3 for ρηματ θεου (by the word of God) as the explanation of creation like Genesis, but here αυτου refers to God's Son as in Hebrews 1:2.

> **Purification of sins** (καθαρισμον των αμαρτιων). Καθαρισμος is from καθαριζω, to cleanse (Matthew 8:3; Hebrews 9:14), here only in Hebrews, but in same sense of cleansing from sins, 2 Peter 1:9; Job 7:21. Note middle participle ποιησαμενος like ευραμενος in Hebrews 9:12. This is the first mention of the priestly work of Christ, the keynote of this Epistle.

Testament, 645.

Sat down (εκαθισεν). First aorist active of καθιζω, "took his seat," a formal and dignified act.

Of the Majesty on high (της μεγαλοσυνης εν υψηλοις). Late word from μεγας, only in LXX (Deuteronomy 32:3; 2 Samuel 7:23, etc.), Aristeas, Hebrews 1:3; Hebrews 8:1; Judges 1:25. Christ resumed his original dignity and glory (John 17:5). The phrase εν υψηλοις occurs in the Psalms (Psalms 93:4), here only in N.T., elsewhere εν υψιστοις in the highest (Matthew 21:9; Luke 2:14) or εν τοις επουρανιοις in the heavenlies (Ephesians 1:3; Ephesians 1:20). Jesus is here pictured as King (Prophet and Priest also) Messiah seated at the right hand of God.[24]

III. Christ is co-glorious with the Father (vv. 4-7)

Being made so much better than the angels, as he hath by inheritance obtained a more excellent name than they. For unto which of the angels said he at any time, Thou art my Son, this day have I begotten thee? And again, I will be to him a Father, and he shall be to me a Son? And again, when he bringeth in the firstbegotten into the world, he saith, And let

---

[24] Robertson, A.T. "*Commentary on Hebrews 1.*" "*Robertson's Word Pictures of the New Testament.*" https://www.studylight.org/commentaries/eng/rwp/hebrews-1.html. Broadman Press 1932,33. Renewal 1960. All subsequent references will be cited as: Robertson, *Word Pictures in the New Testament*, John 3:16 (for example).

all the angels of God worship him. And of the
angels he saith, Who maketh his angels spirits,
and his ministers a flame of fire.

a. *Superiority*

False teachers don't believe Christ is in every
way God, and pagans give adulation to created angels
or messengers. But Hebrews 1 makes it patently clear
that Christ is more superior than the angels (v. 4), and
the subsequent text reveals truth that could never be
said of any angel (v. 5). The author cited Psalm 2:7,
which refers to the reign of the Messiah, and applied
this passage to the person of Christ.

b. *Worship*

As a result of being more excellent than the
angels, the author of Hebrews said, "*proskynesatosan
auto pantes angeloi Theou*" ("let all the angels of God
worship him," v. 6). Giving praise to anyone other
than the one true God is regarded as blasphemy, and
strictly forbidden in Scripture (Exodus 20:5). Isaiah
42:8 says, "I am the LORD: that is my name: **and my
glory will I not give to another**, neither my praise to
graven images" (emphasis mine).

The word *prototokon* or "firstbegotten" has
been the subject of many debates. Arians would argue
firstborn means Christ was created, but not fully
divine. Regarding Hebrews 1:6, scholars have argued
that *prototokon* means supremacy in time or priority
in rank. For example, Bruce asserted that Christ is
called *prototokon* because "he exists before all

creation and because all creation is his heritage."[25] This exposition signifies linguistically that *prototokon* should be interpreted as "a title of honor expressing priority in rank."[26]

Additionally, the author of Hebrews continued his exposition by elevating the supremacy of Christ or His superiority over angels by stating, "And of the angels he saith, 'Who maketh his angels spirits, and his ministers a flame of fire'" (v. 7). Angels were created, but Christ is the creator, and angels are servants, whereas the Son is the Savior!

IV. Christ is called God by the Father (vv. 8-14)

> But unto the Son he saith, Thy throne, O God, is for ever and ever: a sceptre of righteousness is the sceptre of thy kingdom. Thou hast loved righteousness, and hated iniquity; therefore God, even thy God, hath anointed thee with the oil of gladness above thy fellows. And, Thou, Lord, in the beginning hast laid the foundation of the earth; and the heavens are the works of thine hands: They shall perish; but thou remainest; and they all shall wax old as doth a garment; And as a vesture shalt thou fold them up, and they shall be changed: but thou art the same, and thy years shall not fail. But to which of the angels said he at any time, Sit on my right hand, until I make thine

---

[25] Bruce, *The Epistle to the Hebrews*, 56.
[26] Rogers & Rogers, *The New Linguistic and Exegetical Key to the Greek New Testament*, 517.

enemies thy footstool? Are they not all
ministering spirits, sent forth to minister for
them who shall be heirs of salvation?

a. *"o Theos"*

Hebrews 1:8 reveals that Christ is wholly
God, but distinct from the Father. This passage states,
"But unto the Son he saith, 'Thy throne, O God, is for
ever and ever: a sceptre of righteousness is the sceptre
of thy kingdom.'" The Father ("he saith") did not
address the Son as a god, or another god, but literally
referred to the Son as *o Theos* ("the God"). Put
another way, the Son referred to the Father as God
(John 20:17), and the Father also referred to the Son
as God. This doesn't mean Christians believe in many
gods; it means the Father, the Son, and the Spirit
share the same *homoousion.*

b. *"o Theos o Theos sou"*

The subsequent verse also emphasizes the Triunity of God. This passage states, "…therefore **God,
even thy God**, hath **anointed** thee with the oil of
gladness above thy fellows" (v. 9, emphasis mine).
Unitarians cannot account for a text that says, "the
God (o Theos) + even thy (gen. sou) + the God (o
Theos)," but Trinitarians can.

c. Vocative *"Kyrios"*

Again, the author of Hebrews emphasized the
distinction of persons in the Godhead (v. 10). The
noun *Kyrios* is in the vocative case, which means the
Father addressed the Son as *Kyrios* or Lord. This text

poses a serious problem for those who think Christ and the Father refer to the same person.

Additionally, Hebrews 1:10-12 points to Psalm 102:25-27. According to the context of Psalm 102:25-27, one can easily deduce that it refers to the absolute sovereignty of God. Therefore, the Father not only addressed the Son as Lord, but also referred to the Son as the sovereign God in Psalm 102:25-27.

d. *"The **LORD** said unto my **Lord**…"*

The author of Hebrews continued with his defense of the Son's superiority over the angels in Hebrews 1:13 by citing Psalm 110:1. This text states **"The LORD said unto my Lord**, 'Sit thou at my right hand, until I make thine enemies thy footstool'" (emphasis mine).

Since Psalm 110:1 says, "The LORD said unto my Lord…," Jewish scholars will argue that "LORD" points to *Yahweh*, and "Lord" refers to *adoni*, a created being, not *Adonai*, a proper name of God. This argument presupposes that *adoni* has only one meaning, which can easily be refuted in two ways.

First, yes, *adoni* does refer to men (Genesis 18:12; 32:4; 45:8), but it also refers to God, depending on context. According to the *Brown-Driver-Briggs Lexicon*, *adoni* can also be translated as a reference to God:

> **reference to God,** יהוה הָאָדוֹן *the Lord Yahweh* (see H3068 יהוה) Exodus 23:17; Exodus 34:23

(Covenant codes); כָּל־הָאָרֶץ אֲרוֹן *Lord of the whole earth* Joshua 3:11, 13 (J) Psalm 97:5; Zechariah 4:14; Zechariah 6:5; Micah 4:13; צְבָאוֹת יי הָאֲ, earlier Isaiah 1:24; Isaiah 3:1; Isaiah 10:33; Isaiah 19:4 (אֲדֹנָי Isaiah 10:16 in common MT; not Massora, doubtless scribal error); הָאֲ Malachi 3:1; אָדוֹן Psalm 114:7.

reference to God Malachi 1:6; הָאֲדֹנִים אֲדֹנֵי *Lord of lords* Deuteronomy 10:17 = Psalm 136:3; אֲדֹנֵינוּ Psalm 135:5; Psalm 147:5; Nehemiah 8:10; אֲדֹנֵינוּ יי Psalm 8:2 Psalm 8:1; Psalm 8:10 [Psalm 8:9]; Nehemiah 10:30 Nehemiah 10:29; אֲדֹנָיִח יי Isaiah 51:22 (probably = *thy husband, Yahweh*); אֲדֹנָיו Hosea 12:15 [Hosea 12:14] (possibly error for אֲדֹנָי).[27]

Second, the context and exegesis of Psalm 110 indicates that the Lord (*adoni*, v. 1) at the right hand of *Yahweh* is not a created being. Yes, verse 1 says *adoni* is at the right hand of *Yahweh*, but verse 5 reveals that *Adonai* is at the right hand of *Yahweh*. This proves *adoni* and *Adonai* are synonymous or used interchangeably in Psalm 110 to refer to God the Son.

Closing

<hr>

[27] Francis Brown, S.R. Driver, Charles A. Briggs, *The Brown-Driver-Briggs Hebrew and English Lexicon* (Peabody, MA: Hendrickson Publishers), 11, emphasis mine. Reprinted form the 1906 edition originally published by Houghton, Mifflin and Company, Boston. Strong's numberings added by Hendrickson Publishers.

The final verse in the prologue of Hebrew 1 states, "Are they not all ministering spirits, sent forth to minister for them who shall be heirs of salvation?" Examine Gill's exegesis to see how the author of Hebrews elevated the superiority or excellence of Christ over the angels.

Are they not all ministering spirits
Servants to God, to Christ, and to his people, and therefore must be inferior to the Son of God. The phrase is Rabbinical; frequent mention is made in Jewish writings of (trvh ykalm) , "the angels of ministry", or "the ministering angels"; this is their common appellation with the Jews; and the apostle writing to such, uses a like phrase, well known to them, and appeals to them, if the angels were not such spirits.

Sent forth to minister for them who shall be the heirs of salvation?
the persons they minister to, and for, are those, who shall be the heirs of salvation; that is, of eternal glory, which will be possessed by the saints, as an inheritance: hence it belongs to children, being bequeathed to them by their Father, and comes to them through the death of Christ, of which the Spirit is the earnest; and this shows that it is not of works, and that it is of an eternal duration, and takes in all kind of happiness: and of this the saints are heirs now; and so the Ethiopic version renders it, "who are heirs of salvation"; nor should it be rendered, "who shall be heirs", but rather, "who shall inherit salvation"; for this character

respects not their heirship, but their actual inheriting of salvation: and the ministry of angels to, and for them, lies in things temporal and spiritual, or what concern both their bodies and their souls; in things temporal, in which they have often been assisting, as in providing food for their bodies, in curing their diseases, in directing and preserving them in journeys, in saving and delivering them from outward calamities, in restraining things hurtful from hurting them, and in destroying their enemies; in things spiritual, as in making known the mind and will of God to them, in comforting them, and suggesting good things to them, and in helping and assisting them against Satan's temptations; and they are present with their departing souls at death, and carry them to heaven, and will gather the elect together at the last day. And they are "sent forth" to minister to them in such a way; they are sent forth by Christ, the Lord and Creator of them, who therefore must be superior to them; they do not take this office upon themselves, though, being put into they faithfully and diligently execute it, according to the will of Christ: and this shows the care of Christ over his people, and his kindness to them, and the great honour he puts upon them, to appoint such to minister to them; and since they are of so much use and service, they ought to be respected and esteemed, though not worshipped.[28] (Gill, Hebrews 1:14).

---

[28] Gill, *Baptist Commentary Series*, Hebrews 1:14.

This chapter has demonstrated that the preexistent Christ is co-equal, co-eternal, and co-glorious with the Father. As the ultimate agent of creation, Christ rules over all, and thus, all things are in subjection to His sovereign will. This is because Christ is God, but distinct from the Father. Amen.

Chapter 4

The Oneness View of Isaiah 9:6 Debunked

Trinitarians know the Son and the Father are not the same person, nor does the Bible say Christ is "the Father." But since Isaiah 9:6 undoubtedly points to Christ, and refers to Him as "the everlasting Father" (KJV), false teachers think this refutes Trinitarianism, and thus proves Christ and the Father refer to the same *hypostasis*, not distinct persons.

Isaiah 9:6 does not say Jesus is "the Father," nor does it even imply that Christ and the Father refer to the same person. This passage states, "For unto us a child is born, unto us a son is given: and the government shall be upon his shoulder: and his name shall be called Wonderful, Counsellor, The mighty God, **The everlasting Father**, The Prince of Peace" (emphasis mine).

Regarding "the everlasting father," many scholars believe it should be interpreted as Father of an age, Father of all eternity ("'ab ad"),[29] or Father of the world to come ("pater tou mellontos aionos," LXX). The purpose of this chapter is to demonstrate that "the everlasting Father" in Isaiah 9:6 does not support Unitarianism or Oneness theology.

---

[29] See Gary Smith's exegesis of Isaiah 9:6. Gary V. Smith, *The New American Commentary: An Exegetical and Theological Exposition of Holy Scripture. Isaiah 1-39*. Vol. 15A (Nashville, TN: B&H Publishing Group, 2007), 241.

I. Does Isaiah 9:6 say everlasting or eternity (ad)?

The Hebrew *ad* is translated as everlasting, eternity, more, old, or evermore in the OT. But it's presumptuous to affirm any of these translations and apply it to Isaiah 9:6 without examining the context and grammar.[30]

Examining the context and grammar in Isaiah 9:6 is important for two reasons. First, the KJV Bible includes the article ("the"), whereas the Hebrew rendering omits it. Second, many translations use the adjective ("everlasting"), but *ad* is a noun in Isaiah 9:6.

As a noun, *ad* should be understood as eternity, not everlasting. This same noun can also be seen in Isaiah 57:15. This passage states, "For thus saith the high and lofty One that inhabiteth **eternity (ad)**, whose name is Holy…" (emphasis mine). Matthew Poole noted the following about "everlasting Father" in Isaiah 9:6:

> As we render it, the everlasting Father, who, though as man he was then unborn, yet was

------

[30] I watched several videos on Isaiah 9 (via YouTube), and found a few of them to be helpful. For example, I found the following video below to be a concise analysis of Isaiah 9:6, but I do not agree with all of the content. *Does Isaiah 9:6 prove Oneness, that Jesus is God the Father?* Trinity Apologetics. (2015, April 5). Retrieved January 19, 2022, from https://www.youtube.com/watch?v=-NEhVfalqCc&t=557s. Trinity Apologetics is not affiliated in any way with Trinity Gospel Church in Shelbyville, KY.

and is from everlasting to everlasting. They who apply this to Hezekiah render it, the father of an age, and expound this of his long life and numerous posterity; which I the rather mention, to show what absurd shifts they are forced to use who interpret this text of any other but Christ. For he did not live very long, nor had he, that we read of, more than one son, Manasseh. And if both these things had been true of him, they were more eminently true of many other men. **Besides, this Hebrew word being used of God, as here it is of him who was now called the mighty God, constantly signifies eternity, as Isaiah 26:4 57:15, &c.**[31]

II. How should "Father" (ab) be interpreted?

Unitarians or advocates of Oneness theology seem to think "Father" in Isaiah 9:6 only has one definition or refers to the parent of a child. This is far from the truth, so to speak.

Abraham is called *father* (Luke 16:24), Jacob is called *father* (John 4:12), and Isaac is called *father* (Romans 9:10). This does not mean Abraham, Jacob, and Isaac are literally the father of all men without exception.

---

[31] Matthew Poole, *Isaiah*, in *A Commentary On The Whole Bible*. Vol. II: *PSA-MAL* (McLean VA: MacDonald Publishing Company), 347-348, emphasis mine. All subsequent references of Poole's commentaries will be cited as: Poole, *A Commentary On The Whole Bible*, John 15:3 (for example).

Jubal is also referred to as "…the **father** of all such as handle the harp and organ" (Genesis 4:21, emphasis mine). Does this mean Jubal was literally the father of each and every single person who has ever played the harp and organ? Of course not. This is because "father" has more than one meaning.

The word *ab* is primarily translated as father, but it can also refer to a ruler, founder, originator or a term of respect. The *Brown-Driver-Briggs Lexicon* provides an exhaustive overview of *ab*, which needs to be examined:

- *father of individual* Genesis 2:24 (+ אֵם) Genesis 11:28, 29 (twice in verse); Genesis 19:31, 32, 33, + often (mostly J E D); of father as commanding Genesis 50:16 (J) Jeremiah 35:6f, Proverbs 6:20 (compare Genesis 18:19; J Genesis 28:1, 6 P 1 Samuel 17:20; 1 Kings 2:1); instructing מוסר Proverbs 1:8; Proverbs 4:1 (compare Deuteronomy 8:5); specifically as begetter, *genitor* Proverbs 23:22; Zechariah 13:3 (twice in verse) (+ אֵם) Isaiah 45:10; compare Genesis 49:4 (J) Leviticus 18:7, 8, 11 (P); rebuking Genesis 37:10; loving Genesis 37:4; Genesis 44:20 (JE; compare Genesis 22:2; Genesis 25:28; Genesis 37:3; 2 Samuel 14:1); pitying Psalm 103:13 (in simile compare 2 Samuel 18:5); blessing Genesis 27:41 (JE compare Genesis 27:4; also Genesis 28:1 P +); as glad Proverbs 10:1; Proverbs 15:20; compare Proverbs 29:3; grieving Genesis 37:35 (JE; compare 2 Samuel 12:22; 2 Samuel 19:1; 2 Samuel 19:2f) etc. Also as object of honour, obedience, love Exodus

20:12 (E)=Deuteronomy 5:16; Exodus 21:15, 17 (E) Deuteronomy 21:18, 19; Genesis 28:7 (P) 1 Kings 19:20 (all + אֵם), Genesis 50:1; Genesis 50:5 (J) Malachi 1:6 etc. Hence metaphor of *intimate connection* Job 17:14 *to corruption I cry, My father art thou* (‖ לָרְמָה וַאֲחֹתִי אִמִּי).

- **of God** *as father of his people* (see RS[Sem 42]), who constituted, controls, guides and lovingly watches over it: Deuteronomy 32:6; Jeremiah 3:4, 19; Jeremiah 31:9; Isaiah 63:16 (twice in verse); Isaiah 64:7; Malachi 1:6; Malachi 2:10 (compare Exodus 4:22; Exodus 19:4 (JE) Deuteronomy 32:11; Hosea 11:1); compare Jeremiah 2:27 (of idolatrous Israel) יְלִדְתָּנִי: אַתְּ וְלָאֶבֶן אַתָּה אָבִי לָעֵץ אֹמְרִים; especially God as *father of Davidic line* 2 Samuel 7:14; Psalm 89:27; *f. of needy* (late) Psalm 68:6 (compare Psalm 103:13) (in proper name, *father of individual*, compare below)

- ***head of household*, family or clan**; אֲבִי בֵּית as abode Genesis 38:11 (twice in verse); Leviticus 22:13 +; = family Genesis 24:40 (‖ מִשְׁפַּחְתִּי) Genesis 41:51; Genesis 46:31 — Numbers 18:1, 2; Joshua 2:12, 18; Joshua 6:25; especially techn. of divisions of Israel לְמִשְׁפָּחֹת אָב בֵּית Numbers 3:30, 35 = a father's house, i.e. a family or clan; more often plural (בֵּיתאָב אָבוֹת וּתָם, אֲבוֹתָיו) = father's houses = families, clans (compare Di on Exodus 6:14) Exodus 6:14; Exodus 12:3; Numbers 1:2, 18 ff (often in Numbers) Joshua 14:1; Joshua

19:51; Joshua 21:1 (twice in verse); Joshua 22:14 (twice in verse) (always P in Hexateuch); also 1 Chronicles 5:13, 15 + often in Chronicles; compare הלוים אבות ראשֵׁי (= א׳ר בית׳) Exodus 6:25 compare 1 Kings 8:1; 1 Chronicles 6:4; 1 Chronicles 7:11 — Ezra Nehemiah.

- ***ancestor***
    - of individual; grandfather (instead of precise term) Genesis 28:13; Genesis 31:10 [Genesis 32:9] (J; where used by Jacob of Abraham & then of Isaac); greatgrandfather 1 Kings 15:13; great-greatgrandfather 1 Kings 15:11 etc.; oft plural (= *fathers, forefathers*) Genesis 15:15; Genesis 46:34 (JE) 1 Kings 19:4; 1 Kings 21:3, 4; 2 Kings 19:12; 2 Kings 20:17 +; particularly אבותיו עם שכב 1 Kings 1:21; 1 Kings 2:10; 1 Kings 11:21; 1 Kings 22:40 +; joined with אב׳ עם ויקבר 1 Kings 14:31; 1 Kings 15:24; 1 Kings 22:51; 2 Kings 8:24; 2 Kings 15:38 compare 2 Kings 15:7, 2 Kings 16:20 + (all of kings of Judah); intensive, אֲבֹתֶיךָ וַאֲבוֹת אֲבֹתֶיךָ Exodus 10:6 compare Daniel 11:24;
    - of people Genesis 10:21 (J) Genesis 17:4, 5 (P) Genesis 19:37, 38 (J) Genesis 36:9, 43 (P) Deuteronomy 26:5; Isaiah 51:2; Isaiah 43:27 (where הראשׁון אביך *thy first father*, see Che) compare also Ezekiel 16:3, 45 + often; plural Exodus 3:13, 15, 16 (E) Deuteronomy 1:8; Joshua 1:6; Judges

2:1; 1 Samuel 12:6 +; 1 Samuel 12:15.

- *originator* or *patron* of a class, profession, or art Genesis 4:20, 21.

- **figurative of** *producer, Generator* Job 38:28 (מִי־אֶגְלֵי־טָל: אָב (|| הוֹלִיד לַמָּטָר הֲיֵשׁ).

- **figurative of** *benevolence* **& protection** Job 29:6 לָאֶבְיוֹנִים אָנֹכִי אָב, compare Job 31:18; of Eliakim Isaiah 22:21; perhaps also of gracious Messianic king עַד אֲבִי Isaiah 9:5 *everlasting father* (Ge Ew De Che Brd Di) — others *divider of spoil* (Abarb Hi Kn Kue Br[MP]).

- **term of** *respect & honour* (*Abbas, Pater, Papa, Pope*); applied to master 2 Kings 5:13; priest Judges 17:10; Judges 18:19; prophet 2 Kings 2:12 (twice in verse); 2 Kings 6:21; 2 Kings 13:14 (twice in verse); compare 2 Kings 8:9; counsellor Genesis 45:8 (E; compare δευτέρου πατρός add. Esther 3:13; τῷ πατρί 1Mac Esth 11:32); king 1 Samuel 24:12; artificer 2 Chronicles 2:12; 2 Chronicles 4:16.

- **specifically,** *ruler, chief* (late) 1 Chronicles 2:24, 42 (twice in verse); etc. (compare Ew[§ 273 b]) see also Ew[Geschichte. i. 524. H i. 365]. On the force of אָב in proper names (in many probably a divine title), see Che[Ency. Bib., ABI, NAMES WITH] Nö[ib., NAMES, §§ 44, 45] [32].

---

[32] Brown, Driver, Briggs, *The Brown-Driver-Briggs*

As noted above, "father" has more than one meaning. Thus, the context of Isaiah 9:6 ("the everlasting father") indicates that Christ is the founder of eternity. The NT would concur. Christ is God, but distinct from the Father, and is thus the ultimate agent of all creation (John 1:3; Colossians 1:16; Hebrews 1:3). Many scholars would agree.

Matthew Henry believed Christ is the Father of eternity, the author of everlasting life, and the Father of the great work of redemption:

> He is *the everlasting Father,* or *the Father of eternity;* he is God, one with the Father, who is from everlasting to everlasting. He is the author of everlasting life and happiness to them, and so is the Father of a blessed eternity to them. He is *the Father of the world to come* (so the LXX. reads it), the father of the gospel-state, which is put in subjection to him, not to the angels, Heb 2 5. He was, from eternity, Father of the great work of redemption: his heart was upon it; it was the product of his wisdom as *the counsellor,* of his love as *the everlasting Father.*[33]

Gill also argued that Christ, "the Father of eternity," is the author of eternal life, and the everlasting I AM:

Hebrew and English Lexicon, 3, emphasis mine.

[33] Matthew Henry, *Isaiah,* in *Matthew Henry's Commentary on the Whole Bible, Vol. IV, Isaiah to Malachi* (New York, NY: Fleming H. Revell Company, London and Edinburg), 60, emphasis mine. __

Some render the words, "the Father of eternity"; the author of eternal life, who has procured it for his people, and gives it to them; or to whom eternity belongs, who inhabits it, and is possessed of it, is the everlasting I AM, was before all persons and things, was set up in an office capacity from everlasting, and had a glory with the Father before the world was, in whom eternal election, and with whom the everlasting covenant, were made.[34]

Calvin believed in the translation, "the father of the age," and provided a helpful exegesis on *mellontos* and *Father*:

> The father of the age. The Greek translator has added μέλλοντος future; (143) and, in my opinion, the translation is correct, for it denotes eternity, unless it be thought better to view it as denoting "perpetual duration," or "an endless succession of ages," lest any one should improperly limit it to the heavenly life, which is still hidden from us. (Colossians 3:3.) True, the Prophet includes it, and even declares that Christ will come, in order to bestow immortality on his people; but as believers, even in this world, pass from death to life, (John 5:24; 1 John 3:14,) this world is embraced by the eternal condition of the Church.

---

[34] Gill, *The Baptist Commentary Series*, Isaiah 9:6, emphasis mine.

The name Father is put for Author, because Christ preserves the existence of his Church through all ages, and bestows immortality on the body and on the individual members. Hence we conclude how transitory our condition is, apart from him; for, granting that we were to live for a very long period after the ordinary manner of men, what after all will be the value of our long life? We ought, therefore, to elevate our minds to that blessed and everlasting life, which as yet we see not, but which we possess by hope and faith. (Romans 8:25.)[35]

In closing, Isaiah 9:6 does not support Unitarianism, but repudiates it. This passage does not say or even imply that Christ is "the Father."[36]

---

[35] Calvin, J. (2003). *Commentary on the Prophet Isaiah*. (W. Pringle, Trans.) (Vol. VII, Ser. Isaiah, Vol. I). Baker Books, 311. All subsequent references of Calvin's commentaries will be cited as: Calvin, *Commentary On The Gospel According to John,* John 17:3 (for example).

[36] Dr. Dalcour provided a notable conclusion to his exegesis of Isaiah 9:6: "…according to lexical-semantic of **ABIAD (**AB, "father" and AD, "eternal, forever"), the Messiah is the "father," that is, the possessor, source of eternity—the Creator of all things, as the NT indicates (John 1:3; Col. 1:16-17; 1 Cor. 8:6; Heb. 1:2, 10-12; 2:10). **He is the YHWH of Ps. 102:25-27; cf. Heb. 1:10-12**), the unchangeable Creator (He lives forever). But not the person of the Father or Holy Spirit. He is the Son of God (Dan. 7:9-14; Mark 14:61-14; John 5:17-18; 17:5; 2 John 1:3; Rev. 5:13-14)." Dalcour, E. (2018, February 6). *Isaiah 9:6: "Everlasting Father": The Error of Oneness Theology Refuted.* Department of Christian Defense. Retrieved January 19, 2022, from https://christiandefense.org/oneness/isaiah-96-everlasting-father-the-error-of-oneness-theology-refuted/

Instead, Isaiah 9:6 teaches that the preexistent Christ is the ultimate agent, and thus "the mighty God." Created beings are never referred to as "the mighty God" in Scripture, because it's reserved exclusively for God. Amen.

Chapter 5

John 17:3 Supports the Trinity, not Oneness Theology

John 17:3 is often twisted by false teachers. This passage states, "And this is life eternal, that they might know thee the only true God, and Jesus Christ, whom thou hast sent." Instead of embracing the context and exegesis of John 17, false teachers think "only true God" means the Father is God, not the Son.

John 17:3 does not support Unitarianism, but repudiates it. Immediately, one can easily deduce that John 17:3 does not say or even imply that Jesus does not share the same undivided essence of God, nor does it say that only the Father is God, not the Son. Put another way, John 17:3 refutes Oneness theology, and it supports the biblical doctrine of the Trinity. This chapter will explain.

I. Context (John 17:1-2, 4-5)

The whole chapter of John 17 poses serious problems for those who think Christ is an abstraction in the mind of God, or the Father and Son refer to the same person, or Christ is not God. This is because the grammar and context of John 17 proves there are distinct, co-equal, co-glorious, and co-eternal persons in the Godhead. John 17 also defends the preexistence of the Son, and the full deity of Christ.

As a disclaimer, this chapter is not an

extensive or exhaustive review of the whole chapter of John 17. Before addressing John 17:3, this chapter will address a few verses (vv. 1-2, 4-5) in John 17 to demonstrate that one does have not to look far, so to speak, or be a scholar to see the error of Oneness theology.

> **v. 1:** Jesus addressed the *Pater* or Father [vocative, case of address], and spoke in the second person ["thy" ("sou"), "thee" ("se")]. This passage explicitly refers to shared glory between the Father and the Son ["…glorify (doxason) thy (second person) Son, that thy Son also may glorify (doxase) thee (second person)," emphasis mine]. According to the Bible, worshiping anyone or thing other than the one true God is blasphemy, and forbidden (Exodus 20:5; Isaiah 42:8).

> **v. 2:** In His *high priestly prayer* to the Father, Jesus spoke in the second person ["thou has given" ("edokas")]. Created human beings do not have the power to give eternal life. Giving eternal life is a prerogative of the one true God. According to the BDAG lexicon, the adjective *aionion* ("eternal") pertains "…to a period of unending duration, without end."[37]

> **v. 4:** Christ spoke in the first person ["I" ("ego"), "I have finished" ("eteleiosa"), "me" ("moi")], and referred to the Father in the

---

[37] BDAG, *A Greek-English Lexicon of the New Testament and Other Early Christian Literature*, 33.

second person ["thee" ("se"), "thou gavest" ("dedokas")]. Once again, this means Christ and the Father are not the same, but distinct persons.

v. 5: Jesus addressed the *Pater* or Father [vocative or case of address], and He spoke in the first person ["me" ("me"), "I had" ("eixon")]. Additionally, Christ referred to the Father in the second person ["thine own self" ("seauto"), "thee" ("soi")]. According to Wallace, the preposition + dative construction ["with yourself" ("para seauto"), or "with thee" ("para soi")] suggests "proximity or nearness" or association "with someone or something."[38] Christ also referred to the shared glory He had with the Father "before" [prep. "pro"] the world began. This proves Christ is preexistent, fully God, and is co-glorious with the Father.

II. "Life eternal" (John 17:3)

Thus far, it has been shown in John 17 (vv. 1-2, 4-5) that Christ is equally worshiped with the Father, which is nothing new in Scripture (Matthew 14:33; John 1:18; 5:17-19, 23; 8:19; 10:30; 12:44-45; 14:7-11; 15:24; Hebrews 1:3, 6; 1 John 2:23-24; Revelation 5:12-14).

Moreover, John 17:3 says, "**And this is life eternal**, that they might know thee the only true God,

---

[38] Wallace, *GGBB*, 378.

and Jesus Christ, whom thou hast sent" (emphasis mine). Those who say only the Father is God, not Christ, need to explain how they can account for saying Christ is not God if the text says "know thee" ["Father"] *and* "Jesus Christ." Forgiving sins and giving eternal life is attributed to God alone.

John 17:3 does *not* say "this is life eternal, that they know the Father, not the Son." Absolutely not! According to the Bible, the Father forgives sin and gives eternal life, but it also says that Christ forgives sins (Matthew 9:6-8; Mark 2:5-10; Luke 5:20-24; Luke 7:47-49; Acts 5:31), and gives eternal life (John 17:3). Thus, John 17:3 is proof that Christ and the Father are distinct persons, and each person is fully God.

III. "Only True God" (John 17:3)

Unitarians believe "only true God" (John 17:3) is proof the Father is God, but not the Son. But scholars have pointed out that "only true" is not predicated on one person ("thee" or Father), excluding the Son and the Spirit.

John Gill provided an exegetical approach to John 17:3. Gill believed "only true" was not to the exclusion of the Son and the Spirit, but in opposition to the many false gods of the heathens.

The Arians and Unitarians urge this text, against the true and proper deity of our Lord Jesus, and his equality with the Father, but without success; **since the Father is called**

the only true God, in opposition to the many false gods of the Heathens, but not to the exclusion of the Son or Spirit; for Christ is also styled the one Lord, and only Lord God, but not to the exclusion of the Father; yea the true God and eternal life; was he not, he would never, as here, join himself with the only true God; and besides, eternal life is made to depend as much upon the knowledge of him, as of the Father.[39]

Matthew Poole's assessment of "only true God" is similar to Gill's. Poole acknowledged that "only true God" did not exclude the Son and the Spirit, but only false gods:

the only true God. But divines answer, that the term only, or alone, is not to be applied to thee, but to the term God; and the sense this: To know thee to be that God which is the only true God: and this appeareth from 1Jo 5:20, where Christ is said to be the true God, which he could not be if the Father were the only true God, considered as another from the Son. **The term only, or alone, is not exclusive of the other two Persons in the Trinity, but only of idols, the gods of the heathen, which are no gods**; so 1 Timothy 6:15,16, and many other Scriptures: so Matthew 11:27, where it is said, that none knoweth the Son, but the Father; neither knoweth any the Father, save the Son; where the negative doth not exclude

____

[39] Gill, *The Baptist Commentary Series*, John 17:3, emphasis mine.

the Holy Spirit. Besides, the term alone is in Scripture observed not always to exclude all others, as Mark 6:47. Our Saviour saith, it is life eternal to know him who is the only true God, that is, it is the way to eternal life, which is an ordinary figure used in holy writ. He adds,[40]

After reading Gill and Poole's exposition of John 17:3, it is clear that "only true God" is not referring to only one person (Father), excluding the Son and the Spirit. The underlying theme of "only true God" refers to the nature of God.

Yes, the Bible does say, "And this is life eternal, that they might know **thee** the only true God..." (John 17:3, emphasis mine), but it also states that Jesus is equal with the Father (Luke 10:22; John 5:17-23; 10:33; Philippians 2:6; Colossians 2:9; Hebrews 1:3).

Furthermore, Christ is also called "the true God" (1 John 5:20), and the Holy Spirit is referred to

____

[40] Poole, *A Commentary On The Whole Bible*, John 17:3, emphasis mine. Additionally, Calvin noted the following: "The only true God. Two epithets are added, true and only; because, in the first place, faith must distinguish God from the vain inventions of men, and embracing him with firm conviction, must never change or hesitate; and, secondly, believing that there is nothing defective or imperfect in God, faith must be satisfied with him alone. Some explain it, That they may know thee, who alone art God; but this is a poor interpretation. The meaning therefore is, That they may know thee alone to be the true God." Calvin, *Commentary On The Gospel According to John*, John 17:3.

as the true God (Acts 5:3-4). Some will object to these truths.

The exegesis proves Christ is "the true God" in 1 John 5:20. The antecedent of the demonstrative pronoun ("this") refers to "Christ," because "Christ" is immediately followed by "this," and both agree in gender (masculine) and number (singular).

The Bible also proves that the Holy Spirit is the true God. According to Acts 5:3-4, lying to the Holy Spirit is lying to God. The Holy Spirit is omnipotent (Matthew 1:18; Luke 1:35; Ephesians 1:13; 2 Thessalonians 2:13; Titus 3:5), and said things that only God could say (Acts 28:25-27; Hebrews 3:7-11; 10:15-17). This proves the Holy Spirit is God.

Closing

Regarding the "only true God," Christians do not believe in many gods, but the one true God who is multi-personal, i.e., the Father, the Son, and the Holy Spirit. God exists in a plurality of distinct persons, and each person is fully God. Therefore, the Bible teaches that each person in the Godhead is the true God. Amen.

Chapter 6

Emphatic Negation (John 10:28):
A Retort to the Error of Oneness Theology

Advocates of Oneness theology or Unitarians not only deny the Tri-personality of God, but many also reject the doctrine of the perseverance of the saints, and thus believe regenerated Christians can lose their salvation.

God chose the elect, and Christ infallibly secured their salvation; therefore, it is impossible for regenerated Christians to lose their salvation. Remember, Christ said, "…they shall **never perish**, neither shall any man pluck them out of my hand" (John 10:28, emphasis mine).

Regarding the exegesis of John 10:28, the KJV rendering is "…never perish," but the Greek NT uses a double negative *ou me* ("never ever"), and is immediately followed by an aorist subjunctive verb *apolontai* or "perish," which is commonly known as emphatic negation.

The paper will provide insight from notable scholars on emphatic negation [double negative + aorist subjunctive], along with biblical evidence, which poses a major problem for those who believe one can lose their salvation.

**I. Scholarly insight
[doub. neg. + aor. subj]**

David Alan Black, author of *Learn to Read New Testament Greek*, believed the subjunctive of emphatic negation strongly denies that something will happen.

> *The subjunctive of Emphatic Negation.* **The double negative ou μὴ may be used with the *aorist* subjunctive to strongly deny that something will happen**. In this instance, ou μὴ is rendered "certainly not" or "never." Again, the English future is generally used to convey the idea of the Greek construction.[41]

Black believed the subjunctive of emphatic negation should be rendered "certainly not" or "never," and Thayer argued that it signified "…not at all, in no wise, by no means."

> The particles οὐ μή in combination augment the force of the negation, **and signify not at all, in no wise, by no means**; (this formula arose from the fuller expressions οὐ δεινόν or δέος or φόβος, μή, which are still found sometimes in Greek authors, cf. Kühner, ii. § 516, 9, p. 773f; but so far was this origin of the phrase lost sight of that οὐ μή is used even of things not at all to be feared, but rather to be desired; so in the N. T. in Matthew 5:18, 26; Matthew 18:3; Luke 18:17; Luke 22:16; John 4:48; John 20:25; 1 Thessalonians 5:3); cf. Matthiae, § 517; Kühner, ii., p. 775;

---

[41] David Alan Black, *Learn to Read New Testament Greek* (Nashville, TN: Broadman & Holman Publishers, 1994), 164, emphasis mine.

Bernhardy (1829) p. 402ff; (Gildersleeve in the Amer. Jour. of Philol. for 1882, p. 202f: Goodwin § 89): Winers Grammar, § 56, 3 (Buttmann, 211 (183f)).[42]

Black and Thayer's exposition of emphatic negation is similar to one of the most notable Greek resources. According to the BDAG lexicon, the grammatical construction [doub. neg. + aor. subj.] means "never, certainly not…"[43]

Daniel Wallace would agree with "never" or "certainly not." This Greek scholar believed *ou me* + aorist subjunctive is the strongest way to negate something in Greek, and he offered valuable insight on emphatic negation:

> Emphatic negation is indicated by *ou μὴ* plus the *aorist subjunctive* or, less frequently, *ou μὴ* plus the future indicative (e.g., Matt. 26:35; Mark 13:31; John 4:14; 6:35). **This is the strongest way to negate something in Greek**.

> One might think that the negative with the subjunctive could not be as strong as the negative with the indicative. However, while οὐ + the indicative denies a *certainty*, **οὐ μὴ + the subjunctive denies a potentiality**. The negative is not weaker; rather, the affirmative

---

[42] Thayer, *Thayer's Greek-English Lexicon of the New Testament*, 410-411, emphasis mine.

[43] BDAG, *A Greek-English Lexicon of the New Testament and Other Early Christian Literature*, 646.

that is being negatived is less firm with the subjunctive. οὐ μὴ rules out even the idea as being a possibility: "*ou μὴ* is the most decisive way of negativing someth. in the future."

Emphatic negation is found primarily in the reported sayings of Jesus (both in the Gospels and in the Apocalypse); secondarily, in quotations from the LXX. Outside of these two sources it occurs only rarely. As well, a soteriological theme is frequently found in such statements, especially in John: what is negatived is the possibility of the loss of salvation.[44]

Wallace's exegesis on emphatic negation means the grammatical construction in John 10:28 [double negative: *ou* (denies thing) *me* (denies thought) + aorist subjunctive: *apolontai* (denies possibility)] refutes the Oneness view, which teaches that a regenerated Christian can lose their salvation.

Therefore, when the Savior said, "…they shall never ever [double negative: *ou me*] perish [aorist subjunctive: *apolontai*]," one can easily deduce that Christ's grammatical construction denies all possibilities that it will happen in the future.

Additionally, Greek scholar A. T. Robertson said the emphatic double negative in John 10:28 gives security to the sheep for whom Christ died:

---

[44] Wallace, *GGBB*, 468, emphasis mine.

And I give unto them eternal life (καγω
διδωμ αυτοις ζωην αιωνιον). This is the gift of
Jesus now to his sheep as stated in John 6:27;
John 6:40 (cf. 1 John 2:25; 1 John 5:11).

And they shall never perish (κα ου μη
απολωντα). Emphatic double negative with
second aorist middle (intransitive) subjunctive
of απολλυμ, to destroy. The sheep may feel
secure (John 3:16; John 6:39; John 17:12;
John 18:9).

**And no one shall snatch them out of my
hand** (κα ουχ αρπασε τις αυτα εκ της χειρος
μου). Jesus had promised this security in
Galilee (John 6:37; John 6:39). No wolf, no
thief, no bandit, no hireling, no demon, not
even the devil can pluck the sheep out of my
hand. Cf. Colossians 3:3 (Your life is hid
together with Christ in God).[45]

II. Biblical data on
emphatic negation

Thus far, it has been shown that the double
negative + aorist subjunctive means "certainly not,
never, in no way, by no means," and it is the strongest
way to negate something in Greek. Therefore, it's
time to examine a few biblical texts to see that God's
sovereign and indissoluble plan can never be
thwarted.

---

[45] Robertson, *Word Pictures in the New Testament*,
John 10:28, emphasis mine.

Matthew 24:35: "Heaven and earth shall pass away, but my words shall ***not pass away***" [doub. neg. "*ou me*" + aor. subj. "*parelthosin*," emphasis mine].

John 4:14: "But whosoever drinketh of the water that I shall give him ***shall never thirst*…**" [doub. neg. "*ou me*" + aor. subj. "*dipsese*," emphasis mine].

John 6:35: "And Jesus said unto them, 'I am the bread of life: he that cometh to me ***shall never hunger*** [doub. neg. "*ou me*" + aor. subj. "*peinase*"]; and he that believeth on me ***shall never thirst***'" [doub. neg. "*ou me*" + aor. subj. "*dipsese*," emphasis mine].

John 6:37: "All that the Father giveth me shall come to me; and him that cometh to me I will in ***no wise cast out***" [doub. neg. "*ou me*" + aor. subj. "*ekballo*," emphasis mine].

John 11:26: "And whosoever liveth and believeth in me ***shall never die*** [doub. neg. "*ou me*" + aor. subj. "*apothane*"]. Believest thou this" (emphasis mine)?

Romans 4:8: "Blessed is the man to whom the Lord will ***not impute*** sin" [doub. neg. "*ou me*" + aor. subj. "*logisetai*," emphasis mine].

Hebrews 13:5: "Let your conversation be without covetousness; and be content with such things as ye have: for he hath said, I will ***never leave thee*** [doub. neg. "*ou me*" + aor.

subj. "*ano*"], ***nor forsake thee***" [doub. neg. "*ou me*" + aor. subj. "*egkatalipo*," emphasis mine].

Closing

This chapter has shown that scholarship and grammar have refuted the oneness notion of *losing salvation*. As previously stated, no one or thing can stifle God's inviolable plan of sovereign election. This is why Christ said, "…they shall **never perish**, neither shall any man pluck them out of my hand" (John 10:28, emphasis mine). Amen.

Chapter 7

The Spirit is God, but distinct from the Father and The Son

False teachers do not believe the Holy Spirit is God. Oneness theologians will say the Spirit is actually the Father in the mode of the Spirit, and other false teachers will say the Holy Spirit is an impersonal force, not a distinct person, because they think a person denotes a material human being.[46]

This chapter will defend the biblical position that the Holy Spirit is fully God, and is a distinct person in the Godhead. The Holy Scriptures will confirm that the Holy Spirit is not the Father, nor is the Holy Spirit the Son.

I. The Spirit is a distinct person in the Godhead

The Triadic formula in Matthew 28:19 proves the Holy Spirit is a distinct person in the Godhead. This passage demonstrates that each person shares the same case [gen. "Patros" ("Father"), "Uiou" (Son), "Pneumatos" (Spirit)], each case is connected by the conjunction ["kai', ("and")], and each case is articular ["tou" ("the")]. This means each person is not the

---

[46] Those who posit such things have never been able to prove the point they have desperately tried to make; all their psycho babbling proves is that they are either spiritually blind, or intentionally suppressing the truth.

same *hypostasis*, but distinct persons (Granville Sharp Rule).

The gospel of John is saturated with examples, proving the Holy Spirit is not the Father or the Son. In the following texts, Jesus speaks in the first person about the Father and the Spirit in the third person.

> **John 14:16-17:** "And *I* [first person, "ego"] will pray the Father, and ***he shall give*** [third person, "dosei"] you another Comforter, that ***he may abide*** [third person, "mene"] with you for ever. Even the Spirit of truth; whom the world cannot receive, because it seeth him not, neither knoweth him: but ye know him; for ***he dwelleth*** [third person, "menei"] with you, and shall be in you" (emphasis mine).

> **John 14:26:** "But the Comforter, which is the Holy Ghost, whom the Father will send in ***my name*** [first person, "mou"], *he* shall teach you all things, and bring all things to your remembrance, whatsoever ***I have said*** [first person, "eipon"] unto you" (emphasis mine).

> **John 15:26:** "But when the Comforter is come, whom *I* [first person, "ego"] will send unto you from the Father, even the Spirit of truth, which proceedeth from the Father, **he** shall testify of ***me***" [first person, "emou," emphasis mine].

> **John 16:7-8:** "Nevertheless *I* [first person, "ego"] tell you the truth; It is expedient for you that *I* [first person, "ego"] go away: for if

I go [first person, "apeltho"] not away, the Comforter will not come unto you; but if *I depart* [first person, "poreutho"], *I will send* [first person, "pempso"] *him* unto you. And when *he* is come, *he* will reprove the world of sin, and of righteousness, and of judgment" (emphasis mine).

John 16:13-14: "Howbeit when he, the Spirit of truth, is come, *he will guide* [third person, "odegesei"] you into all truth: for *he shall* [third person, "lalesei"] not speak of *himself* [third person, "eautou"]; but whatsoever *he shall hear* [third person, "akouse"], that *shall he speak* [third person, "lalesei"]: and *he will shew* [third person, "anangellei"] you things to come. He shall glorify *me* [first person, "eme"]: for *he shall receive* [third person, "lepsetai"] of *mine* [first person, "emou"], and shall shew it unto you" (emphasis mine).

Additionally, Acts 13:2 says, "As they ministered to the Lord, and fasted, the Holy Ghost said, 'Separate *me* [first person, "moi"] Barnabas and Saul for the work whereunto *I have called* [first person, "proskeklemai"] them'" (emphasis mine). Only a self-aware, rational, and moral person can intelligently say "I" or "me," which refutes those who say the Spirit is not a distinct person in the Godhead.

Paul's apostolic benediction in 2 Corinthians 13:14 also proves there are three distinct and divine persons in the Godhead. In this text, each person shares the same case [gen. "Xristou" ("Christ"), "Theou" ("God"), "Pneumatos" (Spirit)], each case is connected by the conjunction ["kai', ("and")], and each case is articular ["tou" ("the")]. This is another example of the Granville Sharp Rule, which means each noun is distinct, and not the same *hypostasis*.

The Bible is replete with examples on the distinction of persons in the Godhead. Nonetheless, false teachers will insist there are texts that prove the Father and the Spirit are the same person. As an example, many Oneness teachers will say John 4:24 proves God the Father is the Holy Spirit. John 4:24 states, **"God is a Spirit**: and they that worship him must worship him in spirit and in truth."

A simple review of John 4:24 does not teach that the Father is the Spirit, nor does it say "O Theos" ("The God") is "O Pneuma" ("The Spirit"). God is articular, and Spirit is anarthrous ("pneuma o Theos"). *Spirit* has several meanings, not one. Therefore, context and exegesis must determine how Spirit is interpreted.

Additionally, the absence of the article for Spirit does not mean the Father is the Spirit. According to Wallace, "In John 4:24 Jesus says to the woman at the well, pneuma o Theos. The anarthrous PN comes before the subject and there is no verb. Here, pneuma is—stressing the nature or essence of God (the KJV incorrectly renders this, "God is *a* spirit")."[47]

Moreover, the Spirit teaches (John 14:26; 16:8,13-14; Luke 12:12; Acts 8:29; 10:19), testifies

---

[47] Wallace, *GGBB*, 270.

(John 15:26; Hebrews 10:15), commands (Acts 10:19-20; 13:2), and can be grieved (Ephesians 4:30), or blasphemed (Matthew 12:31-32), which are "things that obviously could only be said about a person…"[48]

II. The Holy Spirit is in every way God

The OT and NT teach that the Holy Spirit is a person, not an impersonal force, and is wholly God, but distinct from the Father and the Son. The Bible provides several examples that unequivocally demonstrates that the Holy Spirit is in every way God.

In the OT, the Spirit was an active agent of creation ("…the Spirit of God was hovering over the face of the waters," Genesis 1:2), and is the one who inspired the Holy Scriptures (2 Samuel 23:2; Ezekiel 2:2).

The Holy Spirit gives wisdom and might. Thus, a mighty man or a wise man can never say they gained strength or knowledge on their own, because power and wisdom derive from the Spirit. See Judges 14:6 and Exodus 31:3:

---

[48] Gregory A. Boyd, *Oneness Pentecostals and the Trinity* (Grand Rapids, MI: Baker Book House, 1992), 118. As a disclaimer, Boyd provided a solid defense of the Trinity in this book, but I do not endorse his teachings on the heresy of Open Theism, etc.

Judges 14:6: "*And the Spirit of the LORD came mightily upon him* (Samson), and he rent him as he would have rent a kid, and he had nothing in his hand: but he told not his father or his mother what he had done" (emphasis mine).

Exodus 31:3: "*And I have filled him with the spirit of God*, in wisdom, and in understanding, and in knowledge, and in all manner of workmanship" (emphasis mine).

The Holy Spirit also indwells the elect (Micah 3:8), and spiritually circumcises or regenerates the sheep in His appointed time. An example of regeneration by the Holy Spirit can be seen in Ezekiel 36:25-28:

> Then will I sprinkle clean water upon you, and ye shall be clean: from all your filthiness, and from all your idols, will I cleanse you. A new heart also will I give you, and a new spirit will I put within you: and I will take away the stony heart out of your flesh, and I will give you an heart of flesh. And I will put my spirit within you, and cause you to walk in my statutes, and ye shall keep my judgments, and do them. And ye shall dwell in the land that I gave to your fathers; and ye shall be my people, and I will be your God.

All throughout the Bible, God the Father is absolutely sovereign and eternal, and said things that can only be attributed to the true God. Since the Holy Spirit shares the same undivided essence as the Father and the Son, the Spirit is eternal (Hebrews 9:14) and absolutely sovereign (Matthew 1:18; Luke 1:35; Ephesians 1:13; 2 Thessalonians 2:13; Titus 3:5), and said things that can only be attributed to the true God (Acts 28:25-27; Hebrews 3:7-11; 10:15-17).

The Bible undeniably teaches that the Holy Spirit is God. According to Scripture, the Spirit directs hearts (2 Thessalonians 3:5), indwells (Romans 8:9-11), regenerates (Titus 3:5), sanctifies (2 Thessalonians 2:13), and knows the deep things of God (1 Corinthians 2:10-11).

Furthermore, Acts 5:3-4 says, "But Peter said, Ananias, **why hath Satan filled thine heart to lie to the Holy Ghost**, and to keep back part of the price of the land? Whiles it remained, was it not thine own? and after it was sold, was it not in thine own power? why hast thou conceived this thing in thine heart? **thou hast not lied unto men**, but unto God" (emphasis mine). In summary, verse 3 says Ananias lied to the Holy Ghost, but the subsequent verse says that he lied to God, which means lying to the Holy Spirit is, in fact, lying to God.

Closing

This chapter has demonstrated that the Holy Spirit is a person, not an impersonal force, and is wholly God, but distinct from the Father and the Son. False teachers will reject these truths, but they cannot successfully repudiate it. This is because false teachers will eventually die, but Matthew 24:35 says that God's Word "…shall not pass away" [doub. neg.

"ou me" (denies thing and thought) + aor. subj.
"parelthosin" (denies possibility or potentiality)].

Chapter 8

The True Gospel is Trinitarian

The Father, the Son, and the Holy Spirit are distinct persons in the Godhead, and are thus co-equal, co-eternal, and co-glorious. All three persons in the Godhead are actively involved in the salvation of God's elect. Consequently, there is perfect unity and harmony in the operation of the Godhead.[49]

Regarding the salvation of the saints, the Father chose the elect, the Son died for the elect, and the Spirit seals the elect. Put another way, the *elect* of **God** for whom **Christ** *died* will be *sealed* by the **Spirit**. Therefore, the only way to have perfect unity in the Godhead is to embrace unconditional election, particular redemption, and the sealing of those whom the Father gave to the Son.

I. A false gospel is a denial of the Trinity

False teachers think they believe in the Trinity, yet they embrace a view of the Trinity that teaches that discord or disharmony exists in the operation of the Godhead. This is due to the fact that many embrace unlimited or universal atonement.[50]

---

[49] For more information on perfect unity and harmony in the operation of the Godhead, see Christopher Ness' classic, *An Antidote to Arminianism.*

[50] Rejecting the multi-personality of God is tantamount to rejecting God and His gospel, because the one true God is Tri-personal, and the true gospel is grounded in the doctrine of the Trinity.

As a hypothetical example, the only way false teachers can have perfect unity in the Godhead and consistently say that Christ died for all (without exception) is to also say that God ordained the salvation of all (without exception), and the Spirit seals all (without exception). But this is not what the Bible teaches, and this approach would lead to the heresy of universalism.

The following reasons will explain how false teachers deny the doctrine of the Trinity:

> **The Father:** False teachers will say the Father elected *some* (not all without exception) on the basis of foreseen faith (conditional election), or they will say the Father did not elect anyone at all, but gives everyone libertarian freedom to accept Him.
>
> Nonetheless, these popularly held views do not posit that God elected all (without exception) to be saved, nor do they teach that everyone will profess faith in God. This means false teachers believe only *some* will believe, not all (without exception).
>
> **The Son:** False teachers will say the Son died for all (without exception). This means they believe Christ died for all men, head for head, and soul for soul. Put another way, false teachers believe Christ died for each and every single person who has ever lived in the world.

The Spirit: Unless false teachers are universalists, they would have to say the Spirit only seals those who believe, which refers to *many*, not all men (without exception).

As noted above, false teachers think Christ died for all (without exception), yet they don't believe the Father elected all (without exception), nor do they believe the Spirit will seal all (without exception). According to this view, there is discord or disunity in the operation of the Godhead, which proves false teachers don't believe in the biblical doctrine of the Trinity.

II. The true gospel has perfect unity in the operation of the Godhead

a. The Father ordained the salvation of the elect, not reprobate

False teachers think God's foreknowledge has no causal efficacy, but Paul's exegesis undeniably reveals that those whom the Father foreknew or foreloved will inevitably be glorified. Romans 8:29-30 states:

> For whom he did foreknow, he also did predestinate to be conformed to the image of his Son, that he might be the firstborn among many brethren. Moreover whom he did predestinate, them he also called: and whom he called, them he also justified: and whom he justified, them he also glorified.

According to Romans 8:29-30, the apostle used active verbs, and he concluded with a proleptic or futuristic aorist ("glorified"). Wallace said, "The glorification of those who have been declared righteous is as good as done from Paul's perspective."[51]

Does the Bible teach that God foresaw who would profess their faith in Christ, and He elected them on that basis (commonly called *prescience view*)? Absolutely not! Examine the verbs below:

> **Foreknew:** Examine Romans 8:29, 11:2, and 1 Peter 1:20. God is the subject of the verb *proginosko* [pro: before + ginosko: know], and the object of the verb does not point to one's acceptance of God, but to men. For example, Romans 11:2 says, "God hath not cast away his people which he foreknew." The object of the verb points to "people," not their actions.

> **Chose:** In Ephesians 1:4, the verb *exelexato* ("chose") is in the middle voice, and the object of the verb is the pronoun "us" [viz. elect]. Grammatically, this text does not teach that sinners can choose God, but proves that God chose the elect for Himself.

> **Predestined:** Paul stated, "Having predestinated us unto the adoption of children by Jesus Christ to himself, according to the good pleasure of his will" (Ephesians 1:5).

---

[51] Wallace, *GGBB*, 564.

The verb *proorisas* [pro: before + orizo: determined] is in the active voice, which signifies that God is the one who performed the action, not man.

In summary, God, the prime agent, determined who are His, and no one or thing can thwart His inviolable plan of sovereign election. Therefore, the so-called prescience view should be excoriated, because it elevates men's decisions above the Master's decree.

b. *The Son died for the sheep, not goats*

According to Scripture, God chose the elect, and He gave them to the Son. John 6:37 states, "All that the Father giveth me shall come to me; **and him that cometh to me I will in no wise cast out**" (emphasis mine). This means Christ only died for those whom the Father had given to Him, i.e., the elect.

The gospel teaches that Jesus is in every way God, but distinct from the Father, and the person of the Son became incarnate.[52] He died a substitutionary and propitiatory death for the sheep, not goats, and He resurrected for the elect, not reprobate.

---

[52] Christ is both God and man simultaneously, yet He is not two persons (Nestorian heresy), nor does He have one nature (Monophysitism heresy), nor does He have one will (Monothelitism heresy).

Does the Bible ever say or imply that Christ died for all men without exception? Absolutely not! Examine the following points below:

"It is finished" (John 19:30): According to Thayer, the perfect tense verb *tetelestai* means "everything has been accomplished which by the appointment of the Father as revealed in the Scriptures I must do and bear."[53] Thus, Christ redeemed His sheep from the curse of the law, and the power of Satan, sin, and death. The Savior also propitiated His Father's justice, and He reconciled the elect to God.

John 3:16: This passage does not teach that God loves everyone or that Christ died for all (without exception). On the contrary, John 3:16 teaches that God loves the elect who are believing in Him.[54] "...For [conj: ina] + all [adj: pas] + the [def art: o] + believing [part: pisteuon] + in [prep: eis] + Him [pronoun: auton]."

---

[53] Thayer, *Thayer's Greek-English Lexicon of the New Testament*, 619.

[54] A lot of Arminian street preachers say, "...repent ye, and believe the gospel" (Mark 1:15), but they believe *their faith* saved them, or *their faith* precedes regeneration. So it's no wonder they love to quote and twist this text. They believe their superstitious free will is more superior than the Savior's finished work. Those who argue that *their faith* saved them or *their faith* precedes regeneration are conflating faith and works, which is heresy. Faith is not the ground of justification, but is the instrumental cause, which unites the elect of God to their substitute and Savior, Christ Jesus. Additionally, one's faith and repentance do not merit God's favor, but are gifts that He gives to the elect, after they have been born again.

Particular atonement: In John 10:11, Christ said, "I am the good shepherd: the good shepherd giveth his life *for the sheep*" [prep. "uper" ("for") + def. art. "ton" ("the") + sheep, emphasis mine]. This is not the only time Christ preached on particular redemption in John 10. John 10:15 states, "As the Father knoweth me, even so know I the Father: and I lay down my life **for the sheep**" [prep. "uper" ("for") + def. art. "ton" ("the") + sheep, emphasis mine]. Additionally, Christ told the false teachers that they do not believe in Him, because "...*ye are not of my sheep*, as I said unto you" (John 10:26, emphasis mine).

In summary, Christ said in John 10 that He died for the sheep (v. 11, 15),[55] not all men without exception (v 26). Moreover, Christ also said that His sheep hear and follow Him, and He *knows* them (v. 27). Furthermore, He said that the sheep are the ones who the Father gave to Him (v. 29), and "no man is able to pluck them out of my Father's hand." This is true love! Therefore, when Christ said in Matthew 7:23, "...I never knew you," one can easily see that this was tantamount to Him saying to the false teachers that His Father never gave them to Him, He never died for them, and He never loved them.

---

[55] Christ died for "His people" (Matthew 1:21), and the "church" (Ephesians 5:25). Christ also prayed for the sheep, not goats (John 17:9), and He intercedes for the elect, not reprobate (Romans 8:33-34).

Righteousness of God: 2 Corinthians 5:21 states, "For he hath made him to be sin **for us** [prep. "uper" ("for") + "emon" ("us"); lit., the elect], who knew no sin; that we might be made the righteousness of God in him" (emphasis mine). In this passage, the apostle included himself, meaning he was not referring to all without exception.

What does the righteousness of Christ mean? During the fall (Genesis 3), Adam transgressed the law, and sinned against God. As a result, Adam's sin was imputed to all men without exception. But since God loves the elect, He imputed their sin to Christ, and He imputes the righteousness of Christ to the elect. The righteousness of Christ is the only ground of justification, and assurance of salvation.

Put another way, Adam broke the law, but Christ perfectly kept it. Adam's sin resulted in death, but Christ died for the elect. Thus, the righteousness of Christ refers to His alien preceptive (prefect obedience to the law) and penal obedience (substitutionary/particular death), which is the whole work of the righteousness of Christ in its compact unity.

c. *The Spirit seals the invisible church [viz., elect], not those outside of it*

According to Ephesians 1, the Father chose the elect before the foundation of the world (v. 4), and He predestined the elect (v. 5), according to the good pleasure of His will, to the praise of the glory of His grace (v. 6).

God elected His particular people, and they have "…redemption through his [Christ] blood, the forgiveness of sins, according to the riches of his grace" (v. 7). Since the gospel is grounded in the Trinity, only the elect of God for whom Christ died will be sealed by the Spirit:

> **Ephesians 1:13:** "In whom ye also trusted, after that ye heard the word of truth, the gospel of your salvation: in whom also after that ye believed, *ye were sealed with that holy Spirit of promise*" (emphasis mine).

III. Important disclaimers

God the Father actively reprobated the wicked for hell (Romans 1:28; 9:18, 21-22), and God the Son never purchased goats. Therefore, the Lord hates the wicked (Psalm 5:5), and Christ will castigate them and say, "…I never knew you" (Matthew 7:23).

Asserting that goats can be saved, or opining that reprobates have a chance to repent and believe is imbecilic. Those who disagree failed to read John 12:39-40, which teaches that God actively hardened the hearts and blinded the eyes of the wicked so they could not believe in Him.

Moreover, God's Word never teaches that goats can become sheep, nor does it say that reprobates can become elect, which indicates that the non-elect have no hope of salvation. Knowing these truths does not prevent Christians from witnessing to everyone promiscuously and indiscriminately.

The substitute and Savior said, "…Go ye into all the world, and preach the gospel to every creature" (Mark 16:15). Therefore, it's an indispensable responsibility of every Christian to preach on the person and work of Christ to all without exception.

When the true gospel is preached, the elect will be delivered, but the reprobate will be doomed (1 Corinthians 1:18), in accordance with God's divine sovereignty. May God's will be done!

Furthermore, the Bible does not teach that the Father unconditionally elected Judas, nor does it teach that Christ died for Judas, nor does it teach that Jesus offered to save Judas, nor does it teach that Judas was loved by any person in the Godhead.

Instead, several hundred years before his birth, the Bible prophesied that Judas would betray Christ (Psalm 41:9; 55:12-14, 20-21; Zechariah 11:12-13).

Additionally, Christ referred to Judas as "a devil" (John 6:70), "the son of perdition" (John 17:12), and He said that "…it had been good for that man if he had not been born" (Matthew 26:24).

Therefore, arguing that Jesus loved Judas in any sense or that He tried to save the man [Judas] whom He referred to as "a devil" is intentionally stupefying, and not scriptural.

Closing

This chapter has demonstrated that the true gospel is grounded in the doctrine of the Trinity, and perfect unity exists in the operation of the Godhead. God the Father chose the elect, not reprobate, God the Son died for the sheep, not goats, and God the Spirit seals the invisible church, not those outside of it.

1. All men are born, dead as can be
self-righteous, sinful, and worldly
blinded and unable to see
dead works will never set one free

2. But the Lord is rich in mercy,
one true God, blessed Trinity
the elect will say, "God chose me,"
in accordance with His decree

3. God saves the sheep, not reprobates
His saints are loved, the goats He hates
the wicked won't see heaven's gates,
since they'll be judged, and Hell awaits

4. Chosen by God and justified
elect of God for whom Christ died
eternally loved as His bride
the Spirit seals, He will abide

5. The death of Christ was perfection
God's elect embrace redemption
the saints trust not in wretchedness,
but only in His righteousness

6. The gospel's not an invitation;
it's a sovereign declaration
His finished work, and resurrection,
is why saints can't lose salvation[56]

"Sovereign Grace Hymn"
Written by Sonny Hernandez

---

[56] Sing this hymn to the tune of "Just as I am."

Appendix A

Christological Heresy: Nestorianism

Regenerate believers who take Christology seriously know that the Chalcedonian formulation—two natures united in one person—is not the doctrine of adiaphora; it is an essential of the Christian faith. It is necessary to everlasting salvation that one rightly believes that Christ is *homoousios* [homo: same + ousios: substance] with the Father and is one person or *hypostasis* who has two distinct, unmingled, and inseparable natures.[57]

The Council of Chalcedon (451) repudiated several heresies that attacked the deity of Christ, such as Eutychianism, Apollinarianism, and Nestorianism. Mainly, the controversies were concerning the person of Christ, and His two natures. Thus, the Chalcedonian Creed undeniably and unequivocally teaches that Christ is God of the substance of the Father, and although He is wholly God and wholly man, He is not two, but one person. Take the time to examine the Chalcedonian Creed,

> We, then, following the holy fathers, all with one consent teach men to confess one and the same Son, our Lord Jesus Christ, the same perfect in Godhead and also perfect in

---

[57] This paper was initially published on ReformingAmericaMinistries.com website in January 2020. But since I took the website down to focus on managing my church website, I decided to send this paper to *Sword and Shield*, and they published it in their journal on January 1, 2021.

manhood; truly God and truly man, of a rational soul and body; coessential with the Father according to the Godhead, and consubstantial with us according to the manhood; in all things like unto us, without sin; begotten before all ages of the Father according to the Godhead, and in these latter days, for us and for our salvation, born of the Virgin Mary, the mother of God, according to the manhood; one and the same Christ, Son, Lord, Only-begotten, to be acknowledged in two natures, without confusion, without change, without division, without separation; the distinction of natures being by no means taken away by the union, but rather the property of each nature being preserved, and concurring in one person and one subsistence, not parted or divided into two persons, but one and the same Son, and only begotten, God the Word, the Lord Jesus Christ; as the prophets from the beginning have declared concerning Him, and the Lord Jesus Christ Himself has taught us, and the creed of the holy fathers has handed down to us.

Rejecting the historic Chalcedonian definition of the hypostatic union, which refers to the combination of Christ's two natures in one person, is a foul heresy. One such attack on the divinity of Christ is called Nestorianism. This heresy opposes what was confessionally established at Chalcedon, that the property of each nature being preserved, and concurring in one person. Put another way, the crux of the issue surrounding Nestorianism is that it maintains that Christ is not one person, but is two distinct persons or *hypostases*.

Nestorianism derives its name from Nestorius, a patriarch of Constantinople in 428. Nestorius' Christology was called into question and scrupulously interrogated because he believed that Mary should be called mother of Christ [*Christotokos*; Christ-bearer], and not mother of God [*Theotokos*; God-bearer]. This was due to the fact that Nestorious, like many today, failed to comprehend the hypostatic union, which teaches that the divine *Logos σὰρξ ἐγένετο* ("became flesh"), and is truly God and truly man, not divided into two persons, but one and the same Son, and only begotten, God the Word.

Nestorious was not able to palliate his teachings that Mary was the mother of Christ, not the mother of God, or that Christ was two persons, not one. Nestorius' views on Christology were not only anathematized at the Council of Ephesus (431), but were also condemned as heresy at the Council of Chalcedon (451). Consequently, the Creed of Chalcedon states that Christ was "born of the Virgin Mary, **the mother of God**" (emphasis mine), and in regard to his two natures, it teaches that the property of each nature being preserved, "concurring in **one person** and one subsistence, not parted or divided into two persons, **but one and the same Son**" (emphasis mine).

Even though Nestorianism was condemned as heresy centuries ago, there is a proliferation of professing Christians in the 21st Century who regard Nestorianism as a trivial matter, or a tertiary doctrine that can be overlooked so long as the one propagating the two-person heresy [viz. Nestorianism] is popular. This is due to the fact that many are ignorant about the Tri-personality of God, Christology, and church history, or they simply don't care that the doctrine of the person of Christ is maligned. Examine the following three ways on how to avoid being deceived.

First, Nestorianism is regarded by many scholars as a polysemic term; therefore, Christians should not be surprised when Nestorians are ambiguous or inconsistent in defining their terms. Nonetheless, the crux or the underlying issue of the Nestorian heresy is that it teaches that Christ's deity and humanity were divided and split into two distinct persons living in one body. This is the heresy of Nestorianism that must be rejected.

Second, most modern day heretics who teach a two-person Christ will deny being Nestorians, in the same manner that most heretics will not admit that they teach heresy. Even Nestorious denied that his two-person Christ dogma was erroneous, as many will do today. Therefore, just because one says they are not a Nestorian, Christians should never hastily exonerate them of heresy, unless they unashamedly reject the Nestorian heresy, which taught that the incarnate Christ was two persons, one divine and one human.

Third, don't be duped by Nestorians, either admittedly or not, who try to redefine the meaning of *person* in order to maintain their two-person heresy. A person is an individual *hypostasis* who says "I," and is a moral and rational subsistence that can be distinguished by personal properties.[58] The Bible will concur. For example, the Holy Spirit is called "He" in John 16:13, and the Holy Spirit says, "Me," and "I" in Acts 13:2. In John 14:26, Jesus spoke in the first person ("My") about the Holy Spirit and the Father in the third person.

Additionally, the Bible teaches that the Spirit loves and has fellowship (Romans 15:30; 1 John 1:3); the Spirit commands (Acts 10:19-20; 13:2), and the Spirit grieved (Ephesians 4:30). All three persons of the Godhead can be distinguished by their personal properties: the Father is neither begotten or proceeding; the Son is eternally begotten of the Father before all ages (not made or created), and the Spirit proceeds from both the Father and the Son (see Westminster Confession of Faith).

Therefore, if you meet a Nestorian or read about one that is adamant that previous theologians throughout the church did not properly define the word *person*, don't be duped by their philosophical clap-trap, but realize that their argument does not prove the point they have tried to make; all their argument proves is that they don't like what has been confessionally established and taught throughout Scripture. Christ is never regarded as two persons in the Bible, and albeit He is both truly God and truly man, He is not two persons, but one person, and He is

---

[58] See Hoeksema's definition of a person. Herman Hoeksema, *Reformed Dogmatics*. Second Edition. Vol 1. 2 vols. (Grand Rapids, MI: Reformed Free Publishing Association, 2004), 207.

completely one in the unity of his person, without confusing his natures.

In closing, this paper has explained that it is necessary to everlasting salvation that one rightly believes in the person of the Son, and why Nestorianism is heresy. The controversy surrounding the completeness of Christ's two natures was settled at the Council of Nicea in 325 and Constantinople in 381. Additionally, Nestorianism was condemned as heresy at the Council of Ephesus in 431, but also at the Council of Chalcedon in 451. Therefore, don't be duped by this heresy that was condemned, long ago.[59]

---

[59] Before writing this paper, I read the following material: Athanasian Creed, Nicene Creed, Chalcedonian Creed, and the *Evangelical Dictionary of Theology*. See Griffith, H. (2001). *Nestorius, Nestorianism*. In W. A. Elwell (Ed.), *Evangelical Dictionary of Theology* (Second, pp. 823–824). essay, Baker Academic.

Appendix B

Two Questions for Calvinists who Support John MacArthur's View of Judas Iscariot

In a sermon titled "The Master's Men Part 5: Judas Iscariot,"[60] John MacArthur taught that Jesus loved Judas Iscariot.

Read the sermon manuscript, and you will see that MacArthur said, "Jesus loved him [Judas]" and "He [Christ] was showing love to him [Judas]," and MacArthur argued that Jesus' action toward Judas in giving him the sop at the last supper was "an act of love."

Personally, I reject these unbiblical notions, and if you disagree, respectfully, let's see how you respond to two questions below to determine if you trust in the particular and free grace of God or the false gospel according to John MacArthur.

First Question

Despite MacArthur's love language and teachings about Jesus having loved Judas, where does the Bible explicitly say that Christ loved Judas?

---

[60] John MacArthur, *"The Master's Men Part 5: Judas Iscariot,"* May 31, 1981, retrieved October 30, 2020, from https://www.gty.org/library/sermons-library/2276/the-masters-men-part-5-judas-iscariot.

There are no verses in the Bible that teach that Christ loved Judas. During his incarnate ministry, Christ said that it would have "been good for that man [Judas] if he had not been born" (Matthew 26:24), and Jesus also referred to Judas as "a devil" (John 6:70), but He never said that He loved Judas. Interestingly, MacArthur teaches that Jesus loved Judas, but Jesus called Judas "the son of perdition" (17:12).

Teachers like MacArthur often fail to explain how God can love and hate reprobates simultaneously. The Bible teaches that God "hatest all workers of iniquity" (Psalm 5:5), and "the wicked and him that loveth violence his soul hateth" (11:5).

Arguing that God can love and hate reprobates simultaneously violates the laws of logic. Logic is not a standard that exists apart from God but is an expression of His infinite, eternal, and immutable character. And logic is not contradicting because God is not contradicting. Put another way: logic exists because God exists.

Second Question

Where does the Bible teach that Christ tried to save Judas?

MacArthur teaches that Jesus pleaded with Judas and tried to save him. In an article titled

"Unmasking the Betrayer,"[61] MacArthur said regarding Judas, "Jesus gave him warnings and pleas to bring him to repentance and salvation. And at every point he turned it down. We see that clearly in John 13."

God ordained Judas for eternal destruction; thus, it is absurd to argue that Christ pleaded with Judas to be saved. Several hundred years before his birth, the Bible taught that Judas would be the one who would betray Christ (Psalm 41:9; 55:12–14, 20–21; Zechariah 11:12–13).

According to MacArthur, Jesus was trying to save Judas; but according to the Bible, God the Father ordained Judas for perdition, and God the Son reaffirmed this: "None of them is lost, but the son of perdition; that the scripture might be fulfilled" (John 17:12).

MacArthur taught that Jesus tried to save Judas, but "at every point he turned it down. We see that clearly in John 13." This implies that Christ failed, and Judas could have chosen to be saved and not betray Christ. MacArthur's imbecilic argument should be rejected based on the following:

First, the Bible never teaches that Jesus tried to save Judas, and Christ never fails to save all for

---

[61] John MacArthur, *"Unmasking the Betrayer,"* August 18, 2016, retrieved October 30, 2020, from https://www.gty.org/library/articles/P26/unmasking-the-betrayer.

whom He died. In John 19:30, Christ said, "It is finished." The Greek word $Τετέλεσται$ ("it is finished") is in the perfect tense, which indicates that the action was accomplished or completed once and for all.

Second, the Bible never maintains that Christ loved or tried to save Judas, and it is impossible to argue that Christ was offering salvation to Judas if Christ never purchased salvation for Judas. The Bible teaches that Christ died for the elect (John 10:11), not the goats (v. 26).

Therefore, if the Bible teaches that the gospel is Christ's substitutionary death and perfect obedience that is imputed to God's elect, arguing that Christ tried to save Judas—despite the fact that the Father ordained his perdition and Christ never died and shed his blood for Judas—is tantamount to saying that Jesus was offering a different gospel to Judas.

Moreover, implying that Judas could have chosen to be saved and not betray Christ blatantly ignores the fact that several hundred years before his birth, the OT prophesied that Judas would be the one to betray Christ. Jesus reaffirmed this in John 13:26. This means that it is literally impossible for Judas to have chosen not to be the one who would betray Christ.

Lastly, to argue that Judas had turned down Jesus' pleas of salvation, MacArthur referenced John 13. This is a horrible interpretation of this text. A simple review of John 13 reveals that Jesus never offered Judas salvation, and Jesus knew Judas would betray Him (v. 26). Jesus knew because He is God the Son and is thereby all-knowing and because His Word teaches that Judas would be the one to betray Jesus, as previously discussed. Yes, Judas rejected Christ because God ordained that he would deny Christ, not because Judas turned down Jesus' offer of salvation.

Closing

Regardless of what MacArthur thinks, the Bible does not teach that Christ loved and tried to save Judas. The Bible teaches that Christ loved and died for his elect (Ephesians 5:25), not reprobates. This means that Judas was not loved by Christ, because God ordained his perdition and Christ never died for him.

Thus, Christians need to examine what MacArthur teaches and compare it with the Bible, then remind themselves about Romans 3:4: "*Let God be true, but every man a liar*" (emphasis added).

Appendix C

A Body of Doctrinal Divinity [Chapter 27]: Of a Plurality in the Godhead; Or, a TRINITY of Persons in the Unity of the Divine Essence

By John Gill

Having proved the unity of the divine Being, and explained the sense in which it is to be understood; my next work will be to prove that there is a plurality in the Godhead; or, that there are more persons than one, and that these are neither more, nor fewer, than three; or, that there is a Trinity of Persons in the unity of the divine essence. Some except to these terms, because not literally and syllabically expressed in scripture; as Essence, Unity, Trinity, and Person; of which see the Introduction, see topic (point 5), 741, I shall,

1. First, Prove that there is a plurality of persons in the one God; or, that there are more than one. The Hebrew word phnym which answers to the Greek word prosopa, is used of the divine persons, phny "My persons shall go with thee", (**Exodus 33:14**) and if phnyk "thy persons go not with me, (**Exodus 33:15**) and "he brought thee out vphnyv by his persons", (**Deuteronomy 4:37**). The word is used three times in (**Psalm 27:8, 9**) and in each clause the Septuagint has the word prosopon, and which, as Suidas [149] observes, is expressive of the sacred Trinity. That there is such a plurality of persons, will appear more clearly,

1a. From the plural names and epithets of God. His great and incommunicable name Jehovah, is always in the singular number, and is never used plurally; the reason of which is, because it is expressive of his essence, which is but one; it is the same with "I AM that I AM"; but the first name of God we meet with in scripture, and that in the first verse of it, is plural; "In the beginning God (Elohim) created the heaven and the earth", (**Genesis 1:1**) and therefore must design more than one, at least two, and yet not precisely two, or two only; then it would have been dual; but it is plural; and, as the Jews themselves say, cannot design fewer than three [150] . Now Moses might have made use of other names of God, in his account of the creation; as his name Jehovah, by which he made himself known to him, and to the people of Israel; or Eloah, the singular of Elohim, which is used by him, (**Deuteronomy 32:15, 16**) and in the book of Job frequently; so that it was not want of singular names of God, nor the barrenness of the Hebrew language, which obliged him to use a plural word; it was no doubt of choice, and with design; and which will be more evident when it is observed, that one end of the writings of Moses is to extirpate the polytheism of the heathens, and to prevent the people of Israel from going into it; and therefore it may seem strange, that he should begin his history with a plural name of God; he must have some design in it, which could not be to inculcate a plurality of gods, for that would be directly contrary to what he had in view in writing, and to what he asserts, (**Deuteronomy 6:4**). "Hear, O Israel, the Lord our God is one Lord": nor a plurality of mere names and characters, to which creative powers cannot be ascribed; but a plurality of persons, for so the words may be rendered, distributively, according to the idiom of the Hebrew language; "In the beginning everyone, or each of the divine persons, created the heaven and the earth". And then the historian goes on to make mention of them; who, besides the Father, included in this name, are the Spirit of God, that moved upon the face of the waters, and the word of God, (**Genesis 1:2**) which said, "Let there be light, and there was light"; and which spoke that, and all things, out of nothing; see (**John 1:1-3**). And it may be further observed, that this plural word Elohim, is, in this passage, in construction with a verb singular, "bara", rendered "created"; which some have thought is designed to point out a plurality of persons, in the unity of the divine essence: but if this is not judged sufficient to build it upon, let it be further observed, that the word Elohim is sometimes in construction with a verb plural, as in (**Genesis 20:13; Genesis 35:7; 2 Samuel 7:23**) where Elohim, the gods, or divine persons, are said to cause Abraham to wander from his father's house; to appear to Jacob; and to go forth to redeem Israel: all which are personal actions: and likewise it is in construction with adjectives and participles plural, (**Deuteronomy 4:7, 5:26; Joshua 24:19; 2 Samuel 7:26, 27; Psalm 58:11, Proverbs 30:3; Jeremiah 10:10**) in which places Elohim, gods, or the divine persons, are said to be nigh to the people of Israel; to be living, holy, and to judge in the earth; characters which belong to persons; and now, as a learned man [151] well observes, "that however the construction of a noun plural with a verb singular, may render it doubtful to some whether these words express a plurality or not, yet certainly there can be no doubt in those places, where a verb or adjective plural are joined with the word Elohim". No such stress is laid on this word, as if it was the clearest and strongest proof of a plurality in the Deity; it is only mentioned, and mentioned first, because it is the most usual name of God, being used of him many hundreds of times in scripture; and what stress is laid upon it, is not merely because it is plural, but because it appears often in an unusual form of construction; it is used of others, but not in such a form; as has been observed. It is used of angels, (**Psalm 8:5**) they being not only many, but are often messengers of God, of the divine Persons in the Godhead, represent them, and speak in their name. And it is used of civil magistrates, (**Psalm 82:6**) and so of Moses, as a god to Pharaoh, (**Exodus 7:1**) as they well may be called, since they are the vicegerents and representatives of the Elohim, the divine Persons, the Triune God; nor need it be wondered at, that it should be sometimes used of a single Person in the Deity, it being common to them all; and since each of them possess the whole divine nature and essence undivided, (**Psalm 45:6, 7**). The ancient Jews not only concluded a plurality, but even a Trinity, from the word Elohim [152] . With respect to the passage in (**Numbers 15:16**) they say [153], "There is no judgement less than three"; and that three persons sitting in judgement, the divine Majesty is with them, they conclude from (**Psalm 82:1**) "he judgeth among the gods", 'lhym. Hence they further observes [154], that "no Sanhedrin, or court of judicature, is called 'lhym unless it consists of three". From whence it is manifest, that the ancient Jews believed that this name not only inferred a plurality of persons, but such a plurality which consisted of three at least.

Another plural name of God is Adonim; "If I am

(Adoaim) Lords, where is my fear?" (Mal.. 1:6) now, though this may be said of one in the second and third persons plural, yet never of one in the first person, as it is here said of God by himself; "I am Lords"; and we are sure there are two, "The Lord said to my Lord", &c. (**Psalm 110:1**). In **Daniel 4:17** the most high God is called the watchers and the Holy Ones; "This matter is by the decree of the watchers, and the demand by the word of the Holy Ones"; which respects the revolution and destruction of the Babylonian monarchy; an affair of such moment and importance as not to be ascribed to angels, which some understand by watchers and Holy Ones; but however applicable these epithets may be to them, and they may be allowed to be the executioners of the decrees of God, yet not the makers of them; nor can anything in this world, and much less an affair of such consequence as this, be said to be done in virtue of any decree of theirs: besides, this decree is expressly called, the decree of the most High, (**Daniel 4:24**) so that the watchers and Holy Ones, are no other than the divine Persons in the Godhead; who are holy in their nature, and watch over the saints to do them good; and over the wicked, to bring evil upon them: and as they are so called in the plural number, to express the plurality of them in the Deity; so to preserve the unity of the divine essence, this same decree is called, the decree of the most High, (**Daniel 4:24**) and they the watcher and Holy One, in the singular number in (**Daniel 4:13**).

1b. A plurality in the Deity may be proved from plural expressions used by God, when speaking of himself, respecting the works of creation, providence, and grace. At the creation of man he said, "Let us make man in our image, after our likeness", (**Genesis 1:26**) the pronouns "us" and "our", manifestly express a plurality of persons; these being personal plural characters; as image and likeness being in the singular number, secure the unity of the divine essence; and that there were more than one concerned in the creation of man, is clear from the plural expressions used of the divine Being, when he is spoken of as the Creator of men, (**Job 35:10**; **Psalm 149:2**; **Ecclesiastes 12:1**; Isa.. **54:5**) in all which places, in the original text, it is my Makers, his Makers, thy Creators, thy Makers; for which no other reason can be given, than that more persons than one had an hand herein; as for the angels, they are creatures themselves, and not possessed of creative powers; nor were they concerned in the creation of man, nor was he made after their image and likeness; nor can it be reasonably thought, that God spoke to them, and held a consultation with them about it; for "with whom took he counsel?" (**Isaiah 40:14**). Not with any of his creatures; no, not with the highest angel in heaven; they are not of his privy council. Nor is it to be thought that God, in the above passage, speaks "regio more", after the manner of kings; who, in their edicts and proclamations, use the plural number, to express their honour and majesty; and even they are not to be considered alone, but as connotating their ministers and privy council, by whose advice they act; and, besides, this courtly way of speaking, was not so ancient as the times of Moses; none of the kings of Israel use if; nor even any of those proud and haughty monarchs, Pharaoh and Nebuchadnezzar; the first appearance of it is in the letters of Artaxerxes, king of Persia, (**Ezra 4:18, 7:23**) which might take its rise from the conjunction of Darius and Cyrus, in the

Persian empire, in both whose names edicts might be made, and letters wrote; which might give rise to such a way of speaking, and be continued by their successors, to express their power and glory: but, as a learned man [155] observes, "it is a very extravagant fancy, to suppose that Moses alludes to a custom that was not (for what appears) in being at that time, nor a great while after." The Jews themselves are sensible that this passage furnishes with an argument for a plurality in the Deity [156] . A like way of speaking is used concerning men, in (**Genesis 3:22**). "And the Lord God said, Behold, the man is become as one of us"; not as one of the angels, for they are not of the Deity, nor the companions of God, and equal to him; for whatever private secret meaning Satan might have in saying, "Ye shall be as gods"; he would have it understood by Eve, and so she understood it, that they should be not like the angels merely, but like God himself; this was the bait he laid, and which took, and proved man's ruin; upon which the Lord God said these words either sarcastically, "Behold the man whom Satan promised, and he expected to be as one of us, as one of the persons in the Deity; see how much he looks like one of us! who but just now ran away from us in fear and trembling, and covered himself with fig leaves, and now stands before us clothed with skins of slain beasts!" or else as comparing his former and present state together; for the words may be rendered, "he was as one of us"; made after their image and likeness: but what is he now? he has sinned, and come short of that glorious image; has lost his honour, and is become like the beasts that perish, whose skins he now wears. Philo [157], the Jew, owns that these words are to be understood not of one, but of more; the en kai polla, the "one" and "many", so much spoken of by the Pythagoreans and Platonists; and which Plato [158] speaks of as infinite and eternal, and of the knowledge of them as the gift of the gods; and which, he says, was delivered to us by the ancients; who were better than we, and lived nearer the gods; by whom he seems to intend the ancient Jews; this, I say, though understood by their followers of the unity of God, and the many ideas in him, the same with what we call decrees; I take to be no other than the one God, and a plurality of persons in the Deity; which was the faith of the ancient Jews; so that the polla, of Plato, and others, is the same with the plethos of Philo, who was a great Platonizer; and both intend a plurality of persons.

God sometimes uses the plural number when speaking of himself, with respect to some particular affairs of providence, as the confusion of languages; "Go to, let us go down, and there confound their language"; which also cannot be said to angels; had it, it would rather have been, go "ye", and do "ye" confound their language: but, alas! this work was above the power of angels to do; none but God, that gave to man the faculty of speech, and the use of language, could confound it; which was as great an instance of divine power, as to bestow the gift of tongues on the apostles, at Pentecost; and the same God that did the one, did the other; and so the us here, are after explained of Jehovah, in the following verse, to whom the confounding the language of men, and scattering them abroad on the face of the earth, are ascribed, (**Acts 2:8-11**). In another affair of providence, smiting the Jewish nation with judicial blindness; this plural way of speaking is used by the divine Being; says the prophet Isaiah, "I heard the voice of the Lord saying, Whom shall I send, and who will go for us?" (**Isaiah 6:8**) not the seraphim say this, but Jehovah; for to them neither the name Jehovah, nor the work agree; and though there is but one Jehovah that here speaks, yet more persons than one are intended by him; of Christ, the Son of God no question can be made, since the Evangelist applies them to him; and observes, that Isaiah said the words when he saw his glory, and spoke of him, (**John 12:40, 41**) nor of the Holy Ghost, to whom they are also applied (**Acts 28:25, 26**). There is another passage in **Isaiah 41:21-23** where Jehovah, the King of Jacob, challenges the heathens, and their gods, to bring proof of their Deity, by prediction of future events; and, in which, he all along uses the plural number; "show us what shall happen, that we may consider them; declare unto us things for to come, that we may know that ye, are gods, and that we may be dismayed;" See also **Isaiah 43:9**.

And as in the affairs of creation and providence, so in those of grace, and with respect to spiritual communion with God, plural expressions are used; as when our Lord says, "If a man love me, he will keep my words; and my Father will love him, and we will come unto him, and make our abode with him", (**John 14:23**) which personal actions of coming and making abode, expressive of communion and fellowship, are said of more than one; and we cannot be at a loss about two of them, Christ and his Father, who are expressly mentioned; and hence we read of fellowship with the Father, and his Son Jesus Christ; and also of the communion of the Holy Ghost, (**1 John 1:3; 2 Corinthians 1:14**). To all these instances of plural expressions, may be added (**Song 1:11**; **John 3:11**).

1c. A plurality in the Deity may be proved from those passages of scripture which speak of the angel of Jehovah, who also is Jehovah; now if there is a Jehovah that is sent, and therefore called an angel, and a Jehovah that sends, there must be more persons than one who are Jehovah.

The first instance of this kind is in **Genesis 16:7**, where the angel of Jehovah is said to find Hagar, Sarah's maid, in the wilderness, and bid her return to her mistress; which angel appears to be Jehovah, since he promises to do that for her, and acquaints her with future things, which no created angel, and none but Jehovah could, (**Genesis 16:10-12**) and what proves it beyond all dispute that he must be Jehovah, is, what is said, (**Genesis 16:13**) "She called the name of the Lord, or Jehovah, that spoke unto her, thou; God, seest".

In **Genesis 18:2** we read of three men who stood by Abraham in the plains of Mamre, who were angels in an human form, as two of them are expressly said to be (**Genesis 19:1**). Dr. Lightfoot [159] is of opinion, that they were the three divine Persons; and scruples not to say, that at such a time the Trinity dined with Abraham; but the Father, and the Holy Spirit, never assumed an human form; nor are they ever called angels. However, one of these was undoubtedly a divine Person, the Son of God in an human form; who is expressly called Jehovah, the Judge of all the earth, (**Genesis 18:13, 20, 25, 26**) and to whom omnipotence and omniscience are ascribed, (**Genesis**

18:14, 17-19) and to whom Abraham showed the utmost reverence and respect, (**Genesis 18:27, 30, 31**) and now he is distinguished, being Jehovah in human form on earth, from Jehovah in heaven, from whom he is said to rain brimstone and fire on Sodom and Gomorrah, (**Genesis 19:24**) which conflagration was not made by the ministry of created angels, but is always represented as the work of Elohim, of the divine Persons (**Jeremiah 50:40**; **Amos 4:11**).

An angel also appeared to Abraham at the offering up of his son Isaac, and bid him desist from it; and who appears plainly to be the same with him who ordered him to do it; expressly called God, (**Genesis 22:11, 12** compared with **Genesis 22:1, 2**) and Jehovah, who swore by himself, and promised to do what none but God could do, (**Genesis 22:16-18**; **Hebrews 6:13, 14**) where what is here said is expressly ascribed to God. Add to this, the name Abraham gave the place on this occasion, Jehovah-Jireh, because the Lord had appeared, and would hereafter appear in this place.

The angel invoked by Jacob, (**Genesis 48:15, 16**) is put upon a level with the God of his father's Abraham and Isaac; yea, is represented as the same; and the work of redeeming him from all evil, equal to that of feeding him all his life long, is ascribed to him; as well as a blessing on the sons of Joseph, is prayed for from him; all which would never have been said of, nor done to, a created angel.

The angel which appeared to Moses in the bush, (**Exodus 3:2**) was not a created angel, but a divine person; as is evident from the names by which he is called, Jehovah, God, the God of Abraham, Isaac, and

Jacob, "I AM that I AM", (**Exodus 3:4, 6, 14**) and from the things ascribed to him; seeing the afflictions of the Israelites, coming to deliver them out of Egyptian bondage, and promising to bring them into the land of Canaan, (**Exodus 3:7, 8**) to which may be added, the prayer of Moses for a blessing on Joseph, because of the good will of him that dwelt in the bush, (**Deuteronomy 33:16**) and the application of this passage to God, by our Lord Jesus Christ, (**Mark 12:26**).

Once more, the angel that was promised to go before the children of Israel, to keep and guide them in the way through the wilderness to the land of Canaan, is no other than Jehovah; since not only the obedience of the children of Israel to him is required; but it is suggested, that should they disobey him, he would not, though he could, pardon their iniquities; which none but God can do: and also it is said, the name of the Lord was in him; that is, his nature and perfections; and since it is the same the children of Israel rebelled against, he could be no other than Christ, the Son of God, whom they tempted; the angel of God's presence; who, notwithstanding, saved and carried them all the days of old (**Isaiah 63:9; 1 Corinthians 10:9**).

Again, we read of the angel of the Lord, before whom Joshua the high priest was brought and stood, being accused by Satan, (**Zechariah 3:1**) who is not only called Jehovah, (**Zechariah 3:2**) but takes upon him to do and order such things, which none but God could do; as causing the iniquity of Joshua to pass from him, and clothing him with change of raiment (see **Isaiah 61:10**).

To these may be added, all such scriptures which speak of two, as distinct from each other, under the same name of Jehovah; as in the above mentioned text, (**Genesis 19:24**) where Jehovah is said to rain fire and brimstone from Jehovah, out of heaven; and in **Jeremiah 23:5, 6**, where Jehovah promises to raise up a righteous branch to David, whose name should be called "Jehovah our righteousness"; and in **Hosea 1:7** where Jehovah resolves he would save his people by Jehovah their God. Other passages might be mentioned, as proving a plurality in Deity; but as some of these will also prove a Trinity in it, they will be considered under the following head; where it will be proved,

2. Secondly, That this plurality in the Godhead, is neither more nor fewer than three; or, that there is a Trinity of persons in the unity of the divine essence: this I have before taken for granted, and now I shall prove it. And not to take notice of the name Jehovah being used three times, and three times only, in the blessing of the priest, (**Numbers 6:24-26**) and in the prayer of Daniel, (**Daniel 9:19**) and in the church's declaration of her faith in God, (**Isaiah 33:22**) and the word holy repeated three times, and three times only, in the seraphim's' celebration of the glory of the divine Being, (**Isaiah 6:3**) and in that of the living creatures, in **Revelation 4:8** which may seem to be accidental, or the effect of a fervent and devout disposition of mind; but there is not anything, no not the least thing, that is said or written in the sacred scriptures, without design.

I shall begin with the famous text in **1 John 5:7** as giving full proof and evidence of this doctrine; "For there are three that bear record in heaven, the Father, the Word, and the Holy Ghost; and these three are one": which is not only a proof of the Deity of each of these three, inasmuch as they, are not only said to be "one", that is, one God; and their witness is called the witness of God, (**1 John 5:9**) but of a Trinity of Persons, in the unity of the divine essence; unity of essence, or nature, is asserted and secured, by their being said to be one; which respects not a mere unity of testimony, but of nature; for it is not said of them, as of the witnesses on earth, that they "agree in one"; but that they "are one". And they may be called a Trinity, inasmuch as they are "three"; and a Trinity of Persons, since they are not only spoken of as distinct from each other, the Father from the Word and Holy Ghost, the Word from the Father and the Holy Ghost, and the Holy Ghost from the Father and the Word; but a personal action is ascribed to each of them; for they are all three said to be testifiers, or to bear record; which cannot be said of mere names and characters; nor be understood of one person under different names; for if the one living and true God only bears record, first under the character of a Father, then under the character of a Son, or the Word, and then under the character of the Holy Ghost; testimony, indeed, would be bore three times, but there would be but one testifier, and not three, as the apostle asserts. Suppose one man should, for one man may bear the characters, and stand in the relations of father, son, and master; of a father to a child of his own; of a son, his father being living; and of a master to servants under him; suppose, I say, this man should come into a court of judicature, and be admitted to bear testimony in an affair there depending, and should give his testimony first under the character of a father, then under the character of a son, and next under the character of a master; every one will conclude, that though here was a testimony three times bore, yet there was but one, and not three, that bore record. This text is so glaring a proof of the doctrine of the Trinity, that the enemies of it have done all they can to weaken its authority, and have pushed hard to extirpate it from a place in the sacred writings. They object, that it is wanting in the Syriac version; that the old Latin interpreter has it not; that it is not to be found in many Greek manuscripts; and is not quoted by the ancient fathers who wrote against the Arians, when it might have been of great service to them. To all which it may be replied; that as to the Syriac version, though an ancient one, it is but a version, and till of late appeared a very defective one; the history of the adulterous woman in the eighth of John, the second epistle of Peter, the second and third epistles of John, the epistle of Jude, and the book of Revelation, were all wanting, till restored from a copy of archbishop Usher's, by De Dieu and Dr. Pocock; and who also, from an Eastern copy, has supplied the version with this text, so that now it stands in it. And as to the old Latin interpreter, it is certain that it is to be seen in many Latin manuscripts of an early date, and is in the Vulgate Latin version of the London Polyglot Bible; and the Latin translation which bears the name of Jerom has it; and who, in an epistle to Eustochium, prefixed to his translation of those canonical epistles, complains of the omission of it, by unfaithful interpreters. As to its being wanting in some Greek manuscripts, it need only be said, it is found in many others; it is in the Complutensian edition, the compilers of which made use of various copies; out of sixteen ancient copies of Robert

Stephens's, nine of them had it; and it is also said to be in an old British copy. As to its not being quoted by some of the ancient fathers, this can be no proof of its not being genuine; since it might be in the original copy, and not in that used by them, through the carelessness and unfaithfulness of transcribers; or through copies erased falling into their hands, such as had been corrupted before the times of Arius, even by Artemon, or his disciples, who lived in the second century; who held that Christ was a mere man; by whom it is said [160], this passage was erased; and certain it is, that this epistle was very early corrupted; as the ancient writers testify [161] : or it might be in the copies used by the fathers, and yet not quoted by them, having scriptures not without it, to prove and defend the doctrine of it; and yet, after all, it appears plainly to be quoted by many of them; by Fulgentius [162], in the beginning of the sixth century, against the Arians, without any scruple or hesitation: and Jerom, as before observed, has it in his translation, made in the latter end of the fourth century: and it is quoted by Athanasius [163], about the middle of it; and before him by Cyprian [164], in the middle of the third century: and is manifestly referred to by Tertullian [165], in the beginning of it; and by Clemens of Alexandria [166], towards the end of the second century: so that it is to be traced up within a hundred years, or less, the writing of the epistle; which is enough to satisfy anyone of the genuineness of this text. And, besides, it should be observed, that there never was any dispute about it, until Erasmus left it out in the first edition of his translation of the New Testament; and yet he himself, upon the credit of the old British copy, before mentioned, put it into another edition of his translation. Yea, the Socinians themselves have not dared to leave it out in their German Racovian version, A. C. 1630. To which may be added, that the context requires it; the connection with the preceding verse shows it, as well as its opposition to, and distinction from, the following verse; and in **1 John 5:9** is a plain reference to the divine witnesses in this; for the inference in it would not be clear, if there was no mention before made of a divine testimony. But I shall not rest the proof of the doctrine of the Trinity on this single passage; but on the whole current and universal consent of scripture, where it is written as with a sunbeam; according to which, a Trinity of Persons in the Godhead appears in the works of creation, providence, and grace; in all things respecting the office and work of Christ; in God's acts of grace towards and upon his people; and in their worship and duties of religion enjoined them, and practised by them.

2a. In the works of creation: as by these the eternal power and Godhead are made manifest, so in them are plain traces of a Trinity of persons; that God the Father made the heavens, earth and sea, and all that are in them, under which character the apostles addressed him as distinct from Christ his Son, (**Acts 4:24, 27**) none will doubt; and that the divine Word, or Son of God, was concerned in all this a question cannot be made of it, when it is observed that it is said, "All things were made by him, and without him was not anything made that is made" (**John 1:3**). And as for the Holy Spirit he is not only said to move upon the face of the waters which covered the earth, and brought that unformed chaos of earth and water into a beautiful order, but to garnish the heavens, to bespangle the firmament with stars of light, and to form the crooked serpent, the Leviathan, which being the greatest, is put for all the fishes of the sea; as well as he is said to be sent forth yearly, and renews the face of the earth at every returning spring; which is little less than a creation, and is so called, (**Genesis 1:2**; **Job 26:13**; **Psalm 104:30**) and all three may be seen together in one text, (**Psalm 33:6**) "By the word of the Lord were the heavens made, and all the host of them by the breath of his mouth"; where mention is made of Jehovah, and his Word, the eternal Logos, and of his Spirit, the breath of his mouth, as all concerned in the making of the heavens, and all the host of them. And as in the creation of man, in particular, a plurality has been observed, this plurality was neither more nor fewer than three; that God the Father is the maker of men, will not be objected to; "Have we not all one father? hath not one God created us?" (**Malachi 2:10**) and the Son of God, who is the husband of the church, and the Redeemer of men, is expressly said to be their maker, (**Isaiah 54:5**) and of the Holy Spirit, Elihu in so many words says, "The Spirit of God hath made me, and the breath of the almighty hath given me life" (**Job 33:4**).

2b. A Trinity of persons appears in the works of providence. "My father", says Christ, "worketh hitherto and I work", (**John 5:17**) that is, ever since the works of creation were finished, in which both had an hand, they have been jointly concerned in the works of providence, in the government of the world, and in ordering and disposing of all things in it; and not to the exclusion of the Holy Spirit, for, "Who hath directed the Spirit of the Lord, or being his counsellor hath taught him?" that is, in the affair of the government of the world, as follows; "With whom took he counsel, and who instructed him and taught him in the path of judgement, and taught him knowledge, and showed to him the way of understanding?" to manage the important concerns of the world, to do everything wisely and justly, and to overrule all for the best ends and purposes (see **Isaiah 40:13, 14**). And particularly the three divine persons appear in that remarkable affair of providence, the deliverance of Israel out of Egypt, and the protection and guidance of them through the wilderness to the land of Canaan. Whoever reads attentively (**Isaiah 63:7-14**) will easily observe, that mention is made of Jehovah, and of his mercy, lovingkindness, and goodness to the children of Israel; and then of the Angel of his presence, as distinct from him, showing love and pity to them, in saving, redeeming, bearing, and carrying them all the days of old; and next of his Holy Spirit, whom they rebelled against, and whom they vexed, and yet, though thus provoked, he led them on through the wilderness, and caused them to rest in the land of Canaan.

2c. The three divine persons are to be discerned most clearly in all the works of grace. The inspiration of the scriptures is a wonderful instance of the grace and goodness of God to men, which is the foundation and source of spiritual knowledge, peace, and comfort; it is a divine work: "All scripture is given by inspiration of God", (**2 Timothy 3:16**) of God, Father, Son, and Spirit; and though it is particularly ascribed to the Holy Spirit, "holy men of God spoke as they were moved by the Holy Ghost", (**2 Peter 1:21**) yet no one surely will say, to the exclusion of the Father; nor is there any reason to shut out the Son from a concern herein; and we find all three dictating the writings

David was the penman of: "The Spirit of the Lord spoke by me, and his word was in tongue; the God of Israel said, the Rock of Israel spoke to me", (**2 Samuel 23:2, 3**) where, besides the Spirit of the Lord, who spoke by every inspired writer, there is the Father, the God of Israel, as he is commonly styled, and the Son, the Rock of Israel, the Messiah, often figuratively called the Rock; and in the same manner, and by the same persons David was inspired, all the other penmen of the scriptures were. Those writings acquaint us with the covenant of grace, no other writings do, made from everlasting before the world was; this covenant was made by Jehovah the Father, and was made with his Son, who condescended and agreed to be the surety, mediator, and messenger of it; yea he is said to be the covenant itself; and in which the Holy Spirit is promised, and whose part in it is, and to which he agreed, to be the applier of the blessings and promises of it to those interested therein; see (**Psalm 89:3**; **Isaiah 42:6**; **Malachi 3:1**; **Hebrews 7:22, 12:24**; **Ezekiel 36:27**; **John 16:14, 15**) and they are all three mentioned together as concerned in this covenant, in (**Haggai 2:4, 5**) where, for the encouragement of the people of Israel to work in rebuilding the temple, it is said, "For I am with you, saith the Lord of hosts", according to "the word that I covenanted with you"; or rather, as Junius renders it, "with the Word" by whom I covenanted "with you, when ye came out of Egypt", (at which time the covenant of grace was more clearly and largely revealed;) "so my Spirit remaineth among you": where may be observed, Jehovah the covenant maker, and his Word, in, by, and with whom he covenanted; and the Spirit standing, as it may be rendered, remaining and abiding, to see there was a performance and an application of all that was promised. In the sacred writings, the economy of man's salvation is clearly exhibited to us, in which we find the three divine persons, by agreement and consent, take their distinct parts; and it may be observed that the election of men to salvation is usually ascribed to the Father; redemption, or the impetration of salvation, to the Son; and sanctification, or the application of salvation, to the Spirit; and they are all to be met with in one passage, (**1 Peter 1:2**) "Elect according to the foreknowledge of God the Father, through sanctification of the Spirit, unto obedience and sprinkling of the blood of Jesus". The same may be observed in (**2 Thessalonians 2:13, 14**) where God the Father is said to choose men from the beginning unto salvation; and the sanctification of the Spirit, is the means through which they are chosen; and the glory of the Lord Jesus Christ, the end to which they are chosen and called: but nowhere are these acts of grace more distinctly ascribed to each person than in the first chapter of the epistle to the Ephesians, where God the Father of Christ, is said to bless and choose his people in him before the foundation of the world, and to predestinate them to the adoption of children by him, in whom they are accepted with him, (**Ephesians 1:3-6**) and where Christ is spoken of as the author of redemption through his blood, which includes forgiveness of sin, and a justifying righteousness; which entitles to the heavenly inheritance, (**Ephesians 1:7, 11**) and then the Holy Spirit, in distinction from them both, is said to be the earnest of their inheritance, and by whom they are sealed until they come to the full possession of it (**Ephesians 1:13, 14**). The doctrine of the Trinity is often represented as a speculative point, of no great moment whether it is believed or not, too mysterious and curious to be pried into, and that it had better be let alone than meddled with; but, alas! it enters into the whole of our salvation, and all the parts of it; into all the doctrines of the gospel, and into the experience of the saints; there is no doing without it; as soon as ever a man is convinced of his sinful and miserable estate by nature, he perceives there is a divine person that he has offended, and that there is need of another divine person to make satisfaction for his offences, and a third to sanctify him; to begin and carry on a work of grace in him, and to make him meet for eternal glory and happiness.

2d. A Trinity of persons in the Godhead may be plainly discovered in all things relating to the office and work of Christ, as the Redeemer and Saviour. In the mission of him into this world on that account: he, the Son of God, was sent by agreement, with his own consent, by the Father and the Spirit; this is affirmed by himself, (**Isaiah 48:16**) "Now the Lord God, and his Spirit, hath sent me"; even he who says, (**Isaiah 48:12, 13**) "I am the first and the last", and whose hand laid the foundation of the earth, and whose right hand spanned the heaven, and who is continued speaking to (**Isaiah 48:16**) and must be a divine person; the mighty God, who is said to be sent by Jehovah the Lord God, and by his Spirit; who therefore must be three distinct persons, and not one only; or otherwise the sense must be, "now I and myself have sent myself", which is none at all. Christ the Son of God, sent to be the Saviour, in the fullness of time was made of a woman, or became incarnate; and though he only took flesh, the three divine persons were concerned in this affair; the Father provided a body for him in his purposes and decrees, council and covenant; the Word or Son was made flesh, and dwelt among men, and that which was conceived in the Virgin, was of the Holy Ghost, (**Hebrews 10:5**; **John 1:14**; **Matthew 1:20**) and in the message to the Virgin, and the declaration of this mysterious affair to her by the angel, mention is made distinctly of all the three Persons; there is the "highest", Jehovah the Father; and "the Son of the highest", who took flesh of the Virgin; and the Holy Ghost, or "the power of the highest", to whose overshadowing influence, the mysterious incarnation is ascribed (**Luke 1:32, 35**). Christ, the Son of God, being incarnate, was anointed with the Holy Ghost, his gifts and graces without measure; whereby, as man, he was fitted and qualified for his office as Mediator. The anointer is said to be God, his God, the great Jehovah; the anointed, the Son of God in human nature, called therefore the Christ of God, the true Messiah; what he was anointed with was the Holy Ghost, his gifts and grace, signified by the oil of gladness; see (**Psalm 45:7**; **Isaiah 61:1**; **Acts 10:38**) when he was thirty years of age he was baptized of John in Jordan, where all the three divine persons appeared; the Son in human nature, submitting to the ordinance of baptism: the Father, by a voice from heaven, declaring him to be his beloved Son; and the Holy Spirit, descending on him as a dove (**Matthew 3:16, 17**). This was always reckoned so full and clear a proof of the Trinity of Persons in the Godhead, that it was a common saying with the ancients, go to Jordan, and there learn the doctrine of the Trinity. Before our Lord's sufferings and death, he gave out various promises to his disciples, that he would send the Holy Spirit, the Comforter, to them; in which there are plain traces of a Trinity of Persons; as when he says, "I will pray the Father, and he shall give you another Comforter" (**John 14:16**). Here is God the Father of Christ, who is prayed unto, who is one Person; and here is the Son in human nature, praying, a second Person, the Son of God; and because he was so, his prayer was always prevalent; nor could he be a mere creature, who speaks so positively and authoritatively, he shall give you; and then there is another Comforter prayed for, even the Spirit of truth, distinct from the Father and the Son; the same may be observed in and in (**John 15:26, 16:7**). Christ by his sufferings and death, obtained eternal redemption for men. The price that was paid for it, was paid to God the Father so it is said, "hath redeemed us to God by thy blood" (**Revelation 5:9**). What gave the price a sufficient value was, the dignity of his person, as the Son of God, (**1 John 1:7**) and it was "through the eternal Spirit" he offered himself to God, (**Hebrews 9:14**) which some understand of the divine nature; but it is not usual to say, Christ did this, or the other thing, through the divine nature, but by the Spirit, as in (**Matthew 12:28**; **Acts 1:2**) besides, in some copies of (**Hebrews 9:14**) it is read, "through the Holy Spirit". Again, Christ having suffered and died for men, he rose again for their justification; in which all the three persons were concerned; God the Father raised him from the dead, and gave him glory, (**1 Peter 1:21**) and he raised himself by his own power, according to his own prediction, (**John 2:19**) and was "declared to be the Son of God with power, according to the Spirit of holiness" or the Holy Spirit, "by the resurrection from the dead" (**Romans 1:4**, see also **Rom. 8:11**).

2e. This truth of a Trinity in the Godhead, shines in all the acts of grace towards or in men; in the act of justification; it is God the Father that justifies, by imputing the righteousness of his Son, without works, (**Romans 3:30, 4:6, 8:33**) and it is not only by the righteousness of Christ that men are justified; but he himself justifies by his knowledge, or by faith in him, (**Isaiah 53:11**) and it is the Spirit of God that pronounces the sentence of justification in the conscience of believers; hence they are "justified in the name of the Lord Jesus, and by the Spirit of our God", (**1 Corinthians 6:11**) in the act of adoption; the grace of the Father in bestowing such a favour on any of the children of men, is owned, (**1 John 3:1**) and through the grace of Christ, a way is opened, by redemption wrought out by him, for the reception of this blessing; and he it is that gives power to those that believe in him, to become the sons of God, (**Galatians 4:4, 5**; **John 1:12**) and the Holy Spirit witnesses, their adoption to them; hence he is called the Spirit of adoption, (**Rom. 8:15, 16**) and all three appear in one text, respecting this blessing of grace; "Because ye are sons, God hath sent forth the Spirit of his Son into your hearts, crying, Abba, Father", (**Galatians 4:6**) where the Father is spoken of as distinct from the Son, and the Son from the Father, and the Spirit from them both, and all three bear their part in this wonderful favour. Regeneration is an evidence of adoption; and an instance of the great love and abundant mercy of God; and which is sometimes ascribed to the God and Father of our Lord Jesus Christ, (**1 Peter 1:3**) and sometimes to the Son of God, who regenerates and quickens whom he will, (**John 5:21**; **1 John 2:29**) and sometimes to the Spirit of God, (**John 3:3, 5**) and all three are mentioned together in (**Titus 3:4-6**) where God the Father called our Saviour, is said to save by the washing of regeneration, and the renewing of the Holy Ghost; which grace of his is shed abroad in men through Jesus Christ our Saviour. Once more, their unction, or anointing, which they receive from the Holy One, is from God the Father, in and through Christ, and by the Spirit; "Now he which establisheth us with you in Christ, and hath anointed us, is God; who hath also sealed us, and given the earnest of the Spirit in our hearts", (**2 Corinthians 1:21, 22**) where God the Father is represented as the establisher and anointer, and Jesus Christ, as a distinct person, in whom the saints are established and anointed; and the Spirit, distinct from them both, as the earnest of their future glory.

2f. It plainly appears that there is a Trinity of persons in the Godhead, from the worship and duties of religion enjoined good men, and performed by them. The ordinance of baptism, a very solemn part of divine worship, is ordered to be administered, and is administered, when done rightly, "in the name of the Father, and of the Son, and of the Holy Ghost", (**Matthew 28:19**) which are to be understood, not of three names and characters, but of three persons distinctly named and described, and who are but one God, as the singular word "name", prefixed to them, signifies; men are to be baptised in one name of three persons; but not into one of three names, as an ancient writer [167] has observed; nor into three incarnates; but into three of equal honour and glory. God alone is to be invoked in prayer, and petitions are directed sometimes to one Person, and sometimes to another; sometimes to the first Person, the God and Father of

Christ, (**Ephesians 3:14**) sometimes to Christ himself, the second Person, as by Stephen, (**Acts 7:59**) and sometimes to the Lord the Spirit, the third Person, (**2 Thessalonians 3:5**) and sometimes to all three together, (**Revelation 1:4, 5**) and whereas the saints, who are made light in the Lord, need an increase of light, prayer is made for them, that the God of our Lord Jesus Christ, the Father of glory, would give unto them the Spirit of wisdom and revelation in the knowledge of him, that is, of Christ, (**Ephesians 1:17, 18**) where the Father of Christ is prayed to; the Spirit of wisdom is prayed for; and that for an increase in the knowledge of Christ, distinct from them both: and whereas the saints need an increase of strength, as well as light, prayer is made for them, that the Father of Christ would strengthen them by his Spirit in the inward man, (**Ephesians 3:14-16**; **Zechariah 10:12**) and in a formentioned text, prayer is made to the divine Spirit, to direct the hearts of good men into the love of God, and patient waiting for Christ, (**2 Thessalonians 3:5**) where again the three divine Persons are plainly distinguished; and who may easily be discerned as distinct Persons, in the benedictory prayer of the apostle, (**2 Corinthians 13:14**) with which I shall conclude the proof from scripture, of a Trinity of Persons in the unity of the divine essence; "The grace of our Lord Jesus Christ, and the love of God, and the communion of the Holy Ghost, be with you all". Amen. To which may be added; that a plurality of Persons in the Godhead, seems necessary from the nature of God himself, and his most complete happiness; for as he is the best, the greatest and most perfect of Beings, his happiness in himself must be the most perfect and complete; now happiness lies not in solitude, but in society; hence

the three personal distinctions in Deity, seem
necessary to perfect happiness, which lies in that most
glorious, inconceivable, and inexpressible
communion the three Persons have with one another;
and which arises from the, incomprehensible in being
and unspeakable nearness they have to each other
(**John 10:38, 14:10, 11**).

---

[149] In voce agios.

[150] Vid. Alting. Dissert. Philolog. 4. s. 6, 7, 8.

[151] Allix's Judgement of the Jewish Church, p. 124.

[152] See my Doctrine of the Trinity, p. 30.

[153] Gloss. in T. Bab. Yebamot, fol. 46. 2.

[154] T. Bab. Betacot, fol. 6. 1. & Gloss. in ibid.

[155] Kidder's Demonstration of the Messiah, part 3.
p. 90. edit. fol.

[156] See my Doctrine of the Trinity, p. 35, 36.

[157] tou poiesomen plethos emphainontos, De
Confus. Ling. p. 344, 345.

[158] In Philebo, p. 372, 378. Ed. Ficin. Vid.
Parmenidem, p. 1111, 1112, 1117, 1120, 1122.

[159] Works, vol. 1. p. 13.

[160] Vid. Wittichii Theolog. Pacific. c. 17. s. 254.

[161] Vid. Socrat. Ecclesiastes Hist. l. 7. c. 32.

[162] Respons. contr. Arian. Obj. 10. & de Trinitate, c. 4.

[163] Contr. Arium, p. 109. de Unit. Deitat. Trin. ad Theoph. l. 1. p. 399.

[164] De Unitat. Eccles. p. 255. & in **Ep.** 73. ad Iubajan. p. 184.

[165] Adv. Praxeam, c. 25.

[166] Paedagog. l. 3. in fine.

[167] Ignat. Epist. ad Philip. Ascript. p. 100. Ed. Voss.

Also available on Amazon

The Glorious Triunity of God: *A Family Worship and Bible Study Guide on the Doctrine of the Trinity*

(Available in *Kindle & Paperback*)

About the Author

Sonny Hernandez is pastor of Trinity Gospel Church (KY), and he served 20+ years in the armed forces. He earned a doctorate in pastoral theology/leadership from Tennessee Temple University. He served as an adjunct professor for McKendree University (Radcliff KY Campus) and Grand Canyon University (distance learning). Sonny has authored several books, and has written several published articles for news sources and journals.

TrinityGospelChurchKY.com

ἡ χάρις τοῦ κυρίου Ἰησοῦ
Χριστοῦ καὶ ἡ ἀγάπη τοῦ θεοῦ
καὶ ἡ κοινωνία τοῦ ἁγίου
πνεύματος μετὰ πάντων ὑμῶν